ENCYCLOPEDIA
CORRUPTION
IN THE WORLD

Book 1: Corruption - a Historical Perspective

JUDIVAN J. VIEIRA

authorHOUSE®

AuthorHouse™
1663 Liberty Drive
Bloomington, IN 47403
www.authorhouse.com
Phone: 1 (800) 839-8640

Published by AuthorHouse   04/09/2018

ISBN: 978-1-5462-3277-3 (sc)
ISBN: 978-1-5462-3275-9 (hc)
ISBN: 978-1-5462-3276-6 (e)

Library of Congress Control Number: 2018903374

Print information available on the last page.

This book is printed on acid-free paper.

ACHOWLEDGMENTS

To:

God.

My mother *(in memoriam)* who when I was still a construction labor told me that studying would be the turning point in my life.
Eliane Caetano, my personal assistant and office manager, for the effectiveness and help during the research process and bibliographic organization, for the seven years that made this work a scientific reality and innovative project.

"Thus, to the unjust and intemperate man, it was possible, from the beginning, not to be unjust and intemperate; on which account they are voluntarily so; but when they are become such characters, it is no longer possible for them not to be so; as neither is it possible for him who has thrown a stone, to resume it; at the same time it was in his power to emit from his hand and hurl the stone; for he contained the principle of action in himself."

Aristotle

CONTENTS

PRESENTATION

Arke - Art Representation & Projects, has the honor to introduce you to the First Encyclopedia about Corruption In the World, written by PHD Judivan J Vieira.

Corruption has been such a very important subject all over the world and its importance has been increasing at each blink of eye. There's no society on the world surface that have not tried - at least once in a life time - the taste of it, as a way to handle its own political and economic daily struggles. From the top to the bottom of our globe - and who knows if not beyond – crimes such bribery, exploitation, extortion, fraud, graft, malfeasance and other endless number of illegal practices, have been illustrating some important daily headlines in the most important newspapers out and about.

The use and misuse of this perennial word, which register goes back in times of our history as an unsolved problem, however, has much more in store than we can supposedly wonder. Not even the concept of celestial paradise, the imaginary of perfection capable of bringing the deepest supernatural feeling to all believer human on earth could keep itself out of it.

But, why to talk about corruption? What is corruption indeed? Who's the corrupt and what's its social, political and economic profile? What's the oldest roster in history about it? How history has framed it and how politics have taken their piece of this huge cake artistically decorated with felonious ingredients?

In the attempt to answer all these questions and so many more, Brazilian writer and an intellectual by excellence, Professor Dr Judivan Vieira comes to the table to feed us with such insatiable literary banquet. First published in 2014 in Portuguese, The First Encyclopedia about Corruption in the World brought a new perspective on how to frame the subject, getting away with casuistry by bringing the accuracy of philosophical questions that lead to a better understanding of it, as a selective topic that never ends. From the religious inferences to the contemporary conceptions, the 5 books evolve according to our needs to look at the main plot as a big and complex landscape, having the permission to be persuaded by a profound 101conversation between the author and his reader.

The first book, Corruption - a historical perspective, give us the tools we all need to start a long and intriguing journey towards a world which reveals itself as the face of an old plague, always reinventing itself to fit the historical gaps between now and then. Followed by book two, Corruption - a political perspective, the author digs deep into the world most outstanding theories, exposing philosophers, economists, politicians and all sort of elements that can orchestrate a more comprehensive analysis about the State and its functioning, and Democracy and its main role in this context. Moving on with three other books to complete his magnificent work, professor Vieira uses all his experience as a Federal Prosecutor working with Brazilian Government, to master his audience, showing a remarkable knowledge of his work environment. Legal Perspective of Corruption, International Law Perspective on corruption and Last but not least, Anti-corruption tools in Mercosur and around the world.

We hope all the issues registered, exposed and discussed along these pages – carefully prepared to unveil new perspectives on our thoughts about the theme - can lead you to clarification and a fair attitude before such important matter. Enjoy it!

Joao S Brandao Junior, Arke- Art Representation & Projects's curator

INTRODUCTION

To begin with, we believe it is important to emphasize that the present work is inspired by the research that we have developed for five years for the PhD in legal and social sciences at Universidad del Museo Social Argentino in Buenos Aires, with financing from the Brazilian federal government, through an entity that is part of the indirect public administration; it is also enriched by another two years of research and updating of collected data.

Those research and study years, however, are not enough to exhaust such a complex subject, whose causes, consequences, and allies are purposely hidden from the population, behind the profile of politicians, legislators, and skilled managers in converting truth into lies and injustice in utilitarian justice.

The research work began in 2007, the collection was released in 2014, and the struggle to educate the people to fight against this evil that decimates social well-being must be perennial until we can transform it into substantial public policy.

As you read the books that follow, you will find a surmount of cited work, which I hope does not seem like a show of arrogance or pedantry, but rather the effort to deepen knowledge about the causes, effects, profile of the corrupt, and tools to combat corruption, among other issues and proposals we make.

Research has led us to note that few authors have dared to write specifically about corruption although there are direct and indirect references to it in various sciences and works. In order to fully understand the matter, we read in full more than one hundred and fifty books, as well as economic reports, laws on criminal matters, criminal law and administrative law of the five Mercosur member countries.

We consulted and studied specialized articles and personally attended events such as the Meeting of the Supreme Courts of Mercosur (in Brasilia/

Brazil) and the Foro Unión Europea, América Latina y el Caribe, Las políticas fiscales en tiempo de crisis: volatilidad, cohesión social y economia política de las reformas (Montevideo/Uruguay, 19 y 20 de mayo de 2009).

We are concerned about the quantity and quality of the bibliographic material we have purchased or obtained from a few friends in the various member countries of Mercosur, Spain and the United States of America, to the point of having to set up an office which manages the scheduling of the Federal Attorney General, professor, researcher and writer. This assistance became so important that I decided to keep it indefinitely.

In this theoretical and scientific work, we rely on the thought of George F. Kneller (1980:123) who states, *"Scientific knowledge is expressed through statements and groups of statements of four main types: observations reports, classification schemes, laws and generalizations, and theories."*

Our research was developed based on the above criteria. We made observations, took notes, classified the laws and theories studied, and proposed solutions to the main and secondary problems.

Although we are aware of the fact that it is the first time in human history that the corruption theme is approached in a collection of books, we do not think we are the best nor do we think we can exhaust the subject. We carry the same thought as GUIMARAES, (2002: 32) *"History cannot be concluded as the prevailing truth, nor can it be totally exhausted as much it is pursued by science in this ever changing Universe. There will always be a new trail to be traveled by, which will lead to a number of new considerations."*

What we long for with this research is to shed light in order to help democratic societies realize that corruption related to public goods, monies, and income is a source of impoverishment, and that it drains the forces of the State/Administration and exposes to failure the future of democracy since extreme poverty eventually takes a toll, as mentioned by Professor David S. Landes (1998: xix-xxi):

> "This world is divided roughly into three kinds of nations: those that spend lots of money to keep their weight down; those whose people eat to live; and those whose people don't know where the next meal is coming from. Is the gap still growing today? In extremes, clearly yes. Some countries are not only not gaining, they are growing poorer, relatively and, sometimes, absolutely. Others are

barely holding their own. Others are catching up. Our task (the rich countries), in our own interest as well as theirs, is to help the poor become healthier and wealthier. If we do not, they will seek to take what they cannot make; and if they cannot earn by exporting commodities, they will export people. In short, wealth is an irresistible magnet; and poverty is a potentially raging contaminant: it cannot be segregated, and our peace and prosperity depend in the long run on the well-being of others."

The three kinds of nations mentioned by David Landes are found in the Americas, Asia, Europe, Africa, and Oceania. In 2014, the British NGO Oxfam reported that the world's eighty-five richest people concentrate wealth that exceeds the net worth of 3.5 billion people on the planet.

We agree with Landes when he says that if the poor are united, there is no way for the rich to escape. Behold resentment one day charges its price.

We are aware that men can be studied in the historical, religious, biological, sociological, philosophical, political, economic, and juridical contexts, among others. All these contexts are byproducts of the creative and systematizing capacity of this thinking entity who aims for his or her fulfillment in life.

All things are created and systematized by men and for men, which is why it is up to them to evaluate and reevaluate any institution in order to see if the goal of building social dignity was or was not achieved as planned. If such an institution is a democratic state, it must be effective, otherwise it will have to give way to another institution that really is.

This line of reasoning of a man who creates and systematizes order and "chaos" abstracts from the "Greatest Cause" described by St. Augustine (2000: 175-176) as, "Incorruptible," "Sovereign and the best Good," as described by the creationist theory:

"In this sort did I endeavour now to find out the rest, as I had already found, that was incorruptible must need to be better than that which was corruptible: and thee, therefore, whatsoever thou wert, did I acknowledge to be incorruptible. For never yet soul was, nor ever shall be able to think upon anything which may be better that thou, who art the sovereign and the best good."

Recognizing, further, that all corruptible things are good in their essence, though not absolutely good, Augustine (2000: 187-188) states:

> "Indeed, corruption is harmful, and if it did not diminish good, it would not be harmful. Therefore, either corruption harms nothing - which is not acceptable - or all things that are corrupted are deprived of any good. This is unquestionable."

René Descartes (2000: 35), centuries after Augustine, corroborates this corruptibility in men, asserting that:

"The greatest souls are capable of the greatest vices, as well as of the greatest virtues. (...) From whence it is concluded very clearly that, in spite of the supreme goodness of God, the nature of man, as constituted of spirit and body, can sometimes fail to be fallible and deceitful."

David Hume (2000: 25-26), in turn, speculating on the sentimental man and the rational man sees in human nature an influential being in his evaluations, for the taste and the feeling that the objects awaken to him as influencers of their conduct.

In order to find the governing principles to our understanding, another idea states:

> "MORAL PHILOSOPHY, or science of human nature, can be treated in two different ways ... The first considers man as primarily born for action; as influenced in his evaluations by taste and feeling; pursuing an object and avoiding another, according to the value that these objects seem to possess and according to the light under which they present themselves ... Philosophers of the other class ... consider human nature to be the object of speculation and examine it with strict care in order to find the principles that regulate our understanding, excite our feelings and make us approve or censor any particular object, action or conduct."

Both men (the sentimental and the rational) studied in moral philosophy are active agents in the theory of individual or collective election.

Rupert Pritzl (2000: 99) says that, *"Most corrupt acts are not crimes of passion but crimes of calculation*" and, when analyzing the genesis of public corruption from a micro-economic perspective and describing it in "función de un modelo de elección individual", asserts that:

> "Señalamos oportunamente que una acción corrupta puede ser considerada una decisión individual intencional, adoptada con total racionalidad. A menudo, el autor de típicos delitos económicos es caracterizado como una persona sin sensibilidad comunitaria ni sentido de responsabilidad, un inescrupuloso social cuyo principal objetivo es el enriquecimiento personal. En efecto, hay muchos elementos que indican que los delitos económicos o delitos de 'guante blanco (white collar) obedecen esencialmente a motivaciones económicas. En la génesis de la corrupción pública también puede suponerse una motivación de este tipo."

Rational life is an uncontrollable decision-making process, which is why the theory of individual or collective election is, in our view, one of the most fascinating intellectual elaborations on human nature.

Pritzl (2000: 100-103,106), taken by the ideologies of Heinz Rehkugler and Volker Schindel, writes on the theory of the individual election model, considered a sub-discipline of economic sciences and with full application in any field of knowledge, and says:

> HEINZ REHKUGLER y VOLKER SCHINDEL, definen 'decisión' como selección y realización intencional de una cierta alternativa de acción con vistas a alcanzar un objetivo. En esta definición estricta de 'decisión', se destacan tres elementos centrales: 'intencionalidad', 'variedad de alternativas' y 'realización'. Desde esta perspectiva, decidir significa estudiar las diferentes alternativas, considerar las consecuencias del acto y preverlas mentalmente, intuir cuales serán los beneficios individuales y las probabilidades subjetivas y tomar una decisión en función de la totalidad de las reflexiones hechas. ( )

Dentro de la teoría de la decisión pueden distinguirse una orientación descriptiva y una normativa. La primera de ellas privilegia la descripción de la conducta real y el análisis del proceso de decisión. Su objetivo consiste en explicar cómo se generan las decisiones en la práctica. Por lo tanto, también se habla de teoría de la decisión empírico-realista o teoría de la decisión fáctica. La teoría normativa de la decisión, en cambio, intenta escudriñar y estructurar lógicamente el complejo proceso de decisión, para así ayudar a elegir la mejor opción entre las diferentes alternativas. En este caso también se habla de teoría de la elección racional.

(...)

En el marco de esta teoría es posible diferenciar las situaciones en las que se adoptan las decisiones individuales o colectivas, y clasificarlas según el grado de certeza, riesgo e incertidumbre que presentan (*'estados ambientales'*)

(1) En el caso de las decisiones adoptadas en condiciones de certeza, se conocen de antemano y con absoluta seguridad todas las alternativas posibles, así como sus resultados o efectos.

(2) En el caso de las decisiones adoptadas en condiciones de riesgo, se conocen las diferentes alternativas, pero sus consecuencias son inciertas y sólo pueden inferirse a través de una distribución probabilísima. Los resultados de las diferentes alternativas ya no pueden indicarse en forma terminante, y sólo existe una cierta probabilidad de que una opción escogida traiga consigo determinadas consecuencias

(3) En el tercer caso se trata de decisiones adopta das en condiciones de incertidumbre, situación en que ni siquiera se conocen las probables consecuencias de cada acto específico. En estas circunstancias, el individuo - además de guiarse por reglas generales de acción - suele elaborar por si mismo ciertas probabilidades especificas, estimando de manera subjetiva la posibilidad de que se produzcan determinadas consecuencias. Así se generan

probabilidades subjetivas acerca de los resultados de las respectivas alternativas de acción.

(...)

El siguiente calculo decisional se hará en tres pasos: En una primera etapa se expondrá (1) el incremento espera do de la utilidad, es decir los beneficios que obtendrán los implicados a partir del acto corrupto; en un segundo paso se describirá (2) la perdida esperada de beneficios, es decir el costo que supone la corrupción para los implicados; en un tercer paso se confrontaran por fin (3) lo incrementos esperados de beneficios con las perdidas esperadas, de modo de determinar el beneficio neto o total."

Note that there are three behaviors that drive individual election:

1 - intention;
2 - diversity of alternatives; and
3 - decision.

These behaviors are reflexes of the process of knowledge of the rational man and are expressed in the action or omission directed to specific purpose. This gnoseological process is totally permeated by ethics, by morality, and more recently, by law, a science that created *homo juridicus*.

It is impossible to dissociate the theory of individual or collective election from the conduct of *homo juridicus* because corruption is a phenomenon born of a human act sheltered in the manifestation of free will, which creates the fact punishable by ethics, moral, or the law.

Julio E.S. Virgolini (2004: 28) says with mastery that the realization of human acts is absolutely bound to the will. Here is the excerpt:

"Los condicionamientos del ambiente constituyen fuentes importantes para determinar la disposición o la proximidad de un individuo con la realización de actos desviados, pero el hecho concreto de cruzar la barrera de la conformidad dependerá cada vez más de consideraciones que no son ya susceptibles de ser sometidas a las leyes de la causalidad con el rigor de antaño, puesto que dependen en

última instancia de una decisión a la que se debe reconocer
alguna porción de libertad."

The study of the phenomenon of corruption is indissociable from the study of man himself because talking about man is not always talking about corruption, but it is impossible to talk about corruption without talking about man in his multiple contexts.

At no point in this work do we neglect the fact that Law is far from being the creator of the perfect man. Even though legal norms have assumed in time and space the role of "divine commandments" and the State the role of "God", the law continues to create fantasies that of a "duty" or "must be" distant from the basic needs of man in society.

Carl Schmitt (2006: 46-47) in his *Political Theology* supports the same idea:

> "The battle against traditional religiosity can be traced naturally to many different political and sociological motives: the conservative posture of ecclesiastical Christianity, the alliance of throne and altar, the number of prominent authors who were "déclassé" ( ) Insofar as it retains of the concept of God, the immanence philosophy, which found its greatest systematic architect in Hegel, draws God into the world and permits law and the State to emanate from the immanence of the objective (...) The essence of the State, as that of religion, is mankind's fear of itself."

It is this conscious and free man, active and passive agent of corruption with public assets and monies, who will be exposed in this five-book collection.

We will start from a historical perspective, and we will embody the multiple meanings of the term corruption, its causes and consequences in the public and private sectors, its cost, indices of social perception, the creation of norms and combat institutions in the scope of National, International and Community Law, aiming at demonstrating that corruption continues to impoverish our societies and undermine the foundations of democratic societies.

The focus of the work is corruption with public money in Mercosur, but having in mind the universality of the theme, we offer a panoramic view in the European Union and NAFTA - North American Free Trade Agreement.

We will highlight the intervention of International Public Law through the Inter-American Convention Against Corruption (IACAC) and the United Nations Convention Against Corruption (UNCAC), with the aim of giving a national benchmark to combat the phenomenon about which "experts estimate that about US$ 500 billion in 'dirty money' - about 2% of world GDP - circulate annually in the economy" as reported by the Council For Financial Activities Control (COAF) in the report Money *Laundering, A Worldwide Problem* (1999: 8).

We will present the comparative study that we carried out on the constitutional, criminal, administrative-disciplinary legislation of each member country of Mercosur in order to demonstrate not only similarity but also the possibility of its unification as a means of combating the corruption in these countries.

It is not our intention to propose harmonization of rules of movement of people, goods, services, and capital because this is integration and, as *per se*, it is already a reality in all economic blocks of the world.

What we propose for Mercosur is to take a step forward with the unification of criminal, and administrative-disciplinary legislation, which deals with crimes and acts of improbity committed by public officials with a cross-border reach of each Mercosur public administration once the governments are the projection of the men who govern, as Juan Bautista and Juan de Dios Cincunegui (1996: 15) affirm, based on Machiavelli and Montesquieu thoughts:

"Los gobiernos son la proyección de los hombres que
los gobiernan, e incluso de la propia comunidad gobernada.
El hombre se encuentra plagado de vicios y pasiones, junto
a virtudes y bonanzas – el dilema de los extremos entre
lo horroroso y lo maravilloso de la naturaleza humana."

Just as all human acts and facts relevant to the law depend on a free and conscious will, we firmly believe that if there is will and political-juridical action, we can make use of the existing legislative symmetry and abundantly proven in this work in order to promote unification of criminal, administrative-disciplinary procedures to combat crimes and acts of misconduct by public officials with cross-border reach.

If the political-juridical class really decides to fight against corruption, we will advance to the next stage of our civilizations, which is to provide a substantial democracy to the inhabitants of Mercosur, even creating a paradigm for other peoples, without doubting that the development of the world depends of the development of individuals since it is improving the man who improves the world and, therefore, its institutions.

The purposes announced in philosophy, law, economics, or in any science should be the "common good," that is, the smallest share of well-being to live well in society. We are convinced that social well-being is the basis of happiness.

Corruption has withdrawn from the majority of the world's population the right to a minimum of well-being and, consequently, to "minimum happiness" since when denying education, health, housing, transportation, security, and leisure, mankind is also denied its dignity.

Although public and private information on corruption is mismatched, the general is that the amount disbursed is incommensurable.

For example, "A study carried out by the Department of Competitiveness and Technology (Decomtec) of FIESP (Federation of Industries of São Paulo) revealed the economic and social damages caused to the country by corruption. The total amount reaches 69 billion Brazilian Reais per year."

The Brazilian weekly magazine *Isto é* estimates that the public funds embezzled amounts to 100 billion reais in Brazil only, and, in the world, it exceeds 2.5 trillion reais.

I have no doubt that the fight against corruption must be elevated to the category of substantial public policy before the bankruptcy of the democratic society is established.

After all, what people need is dignity, not formal democracy based on mere legislative promises. Promises and laws are empty manifestations of power and the power I refer to in this work is the power of the State, which is capable of liberating man from ignorance through the educational process, and also free men from other indignities that corruption imposes on our Mercosur people and on various other parts of the world.

The world, in its essence, belongs to the people; public goods and money belong to the people; the right to resistance against corrupt governments also belongs to the people. In order to promote change, it is enough to remember that a little amount of will can be worth more than tons of political-legal fallacy.

BOOK I

Corruption — A Historical Perspective

J.W. Bautista Vidal (1987: 272) states that:

"... ignorance of history condemns people to repeat it. Whether this is true or not, what is important is to know how certain situations evolved, with the aim of predicting it with accuracy, the natural outcome of similar evolutions. This, of course, if timely interventions of intelligence and conscious will do not change their course."

History is a reliable source of the ethical and juridical studies, not meaning that the notion of such sciences has at some point been exhausted by mankind, as affirmed by José Cretella Junior (1968: 19):

> "Literature shows that the notions of ethics and of law
> were not clearly established among Roman jurisconsults,
> which is explained by the direct influence of the Greek
> philosophers upon them."

Despite temporal uncertainties, one of the objectives of mankind must be the eternal persecution of morality, as Immanuel Kant asserted (2000: 484):

> "What use can we make of our understanding, even
> in respect of experience, if we do not propose ends to
> ourselves? But the highest ends are those of morality, and
> it is only pure reason that can give us the knowledge of
> these."

History also exists as a record of the footsteps of man and mankind. We will demonstrate in the following chapters that corruption has followed mankind since the beginning of times.

We will take as paradigm examples of corruption in ancient Greece, ancient Rome, and Judaism, once these three civilizations exert a lot of influence to this day, either by philosophy and way of thinking, or by the practicality of constructing or imitating, as done by the Romans, or by religion that became one of the most influential psychosocial elements of the State.

Professor António Manuel Hespanha (2005 p.101-10), addressing the spontaneously organized character of nature and the order of creation, says:

"In a deeply Christian society, the account of Creation (Genesis, I) cannot fail to play a structural role. There, God appears, fundamentally, giving order to things: separating the darkness from the light, distinguishing the day of the night and the waters of the earth, creating the plants and the animals "according to their species" and giving them different names, appointing things for each other (the herb for the animals, and the fruit for men, man and woman for each other and both for God).

This narrative of Creation - itself resulting from an age-old image of the spontaneously organized character of nature - surely inspired medieval and modern social thought, being explicitly evoked by texts of that time to ground social hierarchies. In the Portuguese Alfonsine Ordinances (1446), this memory of Creation / Ordination appears to justify that the King, in dispensing graces and thereby assigning political and social hierarchies among subjects, did not have treat all the same: *"When our Lord God made creatures, reasonable and those who lack reason, he did not make them to be equal, instead, he established and ordered each one in its individual virtue and power according to the degree he put them in. The same goes for the Kings who in the place of God on earth are put to rule and govern the people in the works they will do - as for justice, as for grace, and as*

for mercy - should follow the example of what he did."
(Alfonsine Ordinances, I, 40)

The academic journey we are making in this first book requires addressing corruption in both the creationist and the evolutionist men, especially because of the knowledge process that shapes them into the multiple relationships they share in society.

CHAPTER 1

Various Meanings Of The Term Corruption

In order to better understand the subject cognitively, we will initially make our research revolve around the multiple meanings of the term corruption, as Ulrich Klug (2004: 112) says: *"Solo la definición precisa de los conceptos que aparecen en las premisas permite practicar inferencias controlables."*

In certain circumstances, in order to conceptualize the "whole" idea, it may be easier when we know the parts that compose it.

Ricardo M. Rojas (1993: 61) is right when he says that *"El término "corrupción" tiene un abanico de acepciones que permiten incluir bajo ese concepto una gran variedad de conductas".*

The word corruption has many meanings, yet its negative essence has not varied much since it has always been conceived as a harmful, denaturalizing conduct of some kind of "good."

Professor Manuel Hespanha (2005: 26), when addressing the transcendence of some words, states:

> "Although many legal concepts or principles are much more modern than is generally supposed, it is true that there are others that seem to exist for a long time with their original meaning (that is, referred to with the same words or as phrases). Indeed, concepts such as people, freedom, democracy, family, duty, contract, property, theft, murder are known as legal constructions since the beginning of European law history."

We can add "corruption" to the group of transcendental words mentioned by Hespanha since it did not change its semantic content. Through time and space, it has actually kept the idea of evil, of deterioration, of decay, of breaking the goodness of something or of someone.

From the lexical point of view, for example, the term corruption takes on the most diverse meanings, such as putrefaction, deviation, alteration, fraud, improbity, error. Under any circumstances is the meaning of the word corruption positive.

There is no conceptual contradiction regarding the conduct of the corrupt. It may be seen as destructive action or omission of what is traditionally, legally, or ethically considered to be just, moral or legal.

Thus, if there is no contradiction of premises, one can believe that the argumentation about the theme is true, as Klug (2004: 207) teaches:

> "La contradicción de premisas hace que una argumentación sea errónea porque, en un sistema de enunciados en el cual tienen validez dos enunciados contradictorios entre sí, ya no se puede distinguir mas entre enunciados verdaderos y falsos."

1.1 – Lexical Interpretation of the Term Corruption

We offer below a lexical conceptualization of the theme in Portuguese, Spanish and English, highlighting its Latin root and its pejorative meaning in all the languages and cultures studied.

In Portuguese

Corrupção (cor.rup.ção) sf (lat corruptione) 1 Ação ou efeito de corromper; decomposição, putrefação. 2 Depravação, desmoralização, devassidão. 3 Sedução. 4 Suborno.

In Spanish

(Del lat. corruptio, -onis). (...) 3. f. Vicio o abuso introducido en las cosas no materiales. Corrupción de costumbres, de voces. 4. f. Der. En las organizaciones, especialmente en las públicas, practica consistente en la

utilización de las funciones y medios de aquellas en provecho, económico o de otra índole, de sus gestores.

In English

Corruption (cor•rup•tion) – noun - dishonest or fraudulent conduct by those in power, typically involving bribery (the journalist who wants to expose corruption in high places); the action of making someone or something morally depraved or the state of being so; the word "addict" conjures up evil and corruption; archaic decay; putrefaction (the potato turned black and rotten with corruption).

1.2 – Juridical-Doctrinal Interpretation on Corruption

Mariano Grondona (1993: 20) says that:

> "La raíz indoeuropea de la palabra 'corrupción' es reut, que quiere decir 'arrebatar'. La primera definición que de este verbo da El diccionario de La Real Academia Española ES 'quitar o tomar alguna cosa con violencia y fuerza (...) si en cambio, corrompo a un menor, lo privo de su integridad: le arrebato su naturaleza (...) Corromper es pues desnaturalizar, desviar una cosa del fin hacia el cual naturalmente tiende (...)' Si los mecanismos del Estado están infiltrados por la corrupción en el sector publico es más grave que la privada..."

Grondona (1993: 21) considers that there are three degrees of corruption:

> "El primer grado es el de la propina o regalo que se ofrece como signo de gentileza o gratitud. El segundo grado es la exacción, esto es, la extorsión de un funcionario a un ciudadano para que pague por obtener lo que, de todos modos, le es debido. Por último, existe el cohecho, pago que se ofrece o se da para que un funcionario haga lo que no es debido."

In mathematics, degree is the order number that expresses the number of factors of the same species. By analogy, in this book, the term "species" of corruption will be used, without hierarchy, recognizing that the whole is formed by elements, that is, that corruption is a genre in which we can identify varied species, without deviating from the focal idea which is corruption with public goods, monies and revenues.

David Baigun (2006: 115-116) when analyzing the multiple meanings of the word corruption, says:

"La palabra corrupción tiene diferentes acepciones.
En orden cronológico:

a) arruinado, contaminado y podrido;
b) divergente o desviado respecto del standard moral, pervertido e se viera reflejado en los distintos códigos penales em los delitos sexuales;
c) venal, apropiación de recursos y privilegios, a través del pago y recepción de aquellos que tienen poder de decisión y influencia en la distribución de los mismos (reflejándose en los códigos penales en los delitos contra la administración pública)"
(...)

"Carlos Nino agrupo las definiciones existentes desde el siguiente enfoque:

a) Centradas en su relación con la función pública (Bayley). Comprendiendo los casos de nombramientos de familiares o terceras personas por favores o compromisos anteriores (acomodos o ganchos).
b) Centradas en el mercado (Van Kleveren). En el cual el funcionario utiliza su posición de privilegio como una manera de hacer negocios, desapareciendo aquello de ser un servidor público.
c) Centradas en el interés público (Friedrich). Aquí el funcionario responsable es inducido, por incentivos monetarios o de otro carácter, a beneficiar a quien ofrece los incentivos y causa, por lo tanto, daño al público y sus intereses."

Baigun interprets corruption as a moral deviation and coincides with Carlos Niño when he correlates it to a deviance of functional conduct, in which a public official uses his or her function to achieve personal advantage, to the detriment of collective interest.

This can happen when an employee wishes to privilege kinship, when he uses his position as the bargaining chip in the public-private business world, or when the public agent corrupts or allows himself to be corrupted to benefit third parties.

1.3 – Political Science Interpretation on Corruption

Professor of the University of Pisa, Antonio A. Martino describes corruption as a threat to democracy. He asserts that democracy is not made of thieves, but if they are not fought they can take democracy to its overthrow. Here is what he says:

> "Cuando una sociedad comienza a admitir que se violen algunas normas éticas y jurídicas por una suerte de realismo político (cosi fan tutte) no solo admite que algunos roben descaradamente más que otros porque son mas sinvergüenzas o porque tuvieron mejores oportunidades, sino que poco a poco justifican la propia violación de las reglas, ahora en base a una suerte de realismo social, por el cual el que no llora no mama y el que no mama es un gil. A esa altura se está jugando a otro juego, que consiste en no aceptar seguir las reglas sino aparentemente y en cuanto convenga.

> No hay democracias de ladrones, hay ladrones que sí tolerados, desbaratarán antes o después la democracia."

There is no democracy of thieves, but thieves who, if tolerated, sooner or later will ruin democracy.

Juan Carlos Ferre Olive (2002:229), when quoting Joao Davin, states that"

> "La corrupción inunda todas las manifestaciones sociales, agrediendo los intereses más esenciales del ciudadano

en beneficio de quienes detentan el poder. Refiriéndose a la desastrosa situación existente en gran parte de África, el Secretario General de Naciones Unidas, Kofi Annan, declaraba que 'el hambre la guerra, el sida (...) no desaparecerán mientras el poder siga en manos de gobernantes corruptos que solo piensan en sus intereses personales.' Eduardo Fabian Caparros, La Corrupción Aspectos Jurídicos y Económicos, Ratio Legis, Salamanca, 2000, Page 20."

United Nations Secretary-General Kofi Annan rightly asserted that hunger, war, and AIDS will never go away as long as power is in the hands of corrupt governments. The reason for believing that Kofi Annan's statement is true stems from the simple fact that corrupt governments only aim at their interests being one of their principal interests to perpetuate themselves in power.

During a speech at "*Asociacion de magistrados del Uruguay*" (1998:17), Eduardo Cavalli elaborated on the concept of corruption and handled well the variables or premises that integrate such conduct, as follows:

"Por tanto podemos ir sentando un concepto más o menos aproximado de la corrupción en base a estas premisas:

- se trata de una agresión al orden instituido par la naturaleza o par ley, de las cosas;
- la agresión refiere a la cosa pública, particularmente a la labor del Estado, sea en servicios esenciales, públicos o en la labor que realiza el Estado irrumpiendo en actividades de naturaleza privada que el Estado asume o en las que ejerce algún tipo de control;
- no es necesario para el fenómeno de la corrupción que se trate de agresiones conocidas como de cuello blanco o de delitos macro económicos sino que puede referirse a actividades cuyo daño es de menor entidad económica o incluso de significación no económica.
- esa agresión se caracteriza también por sus consecuencias:
- por un lado, hecha a perder en mayor o menor parte a las instituciones.

- por otro, supone una incorrección de las personas quo tienen como deber la salvaguarda de las instituciones y su moralidad;
- en tercer lugar provoca en el medio social la pérdida de confianza en esas instituciones y en los hombres que participan en ella."

In short, Eduardo Cavalli says that corruption is:
1 - an aggression to order instituted by nature;
2 - an aggression against the State, with the consequence of ruining its institutions and its credibility.

1.4 – Corruption as a Betrayal of Legality

Juan Bautista and Juan de Dios Cincunegui (1996: 18), quoting Adolfo Saban Godoy affirm *"que la corrupción es una traición fundamental de los deberes de lealtad, probidad y fidelidad de la función pública"*.

Guillermo Ariel Todarello (2008: 112, 115-116, 119) lists the following aspects of the corruption phenomenon:

"IV. 1. Corrupción nacional y transnacional

De acuerdo con el marco en el cual se desarrolle el acto o el sistema de corrupción, es importante distinguir entre la corrupción desplegada a nivel nacional, es decir, aquella constituida por actos irregulares acaecidos en el ámbito gubernamental limitado a un Estado en particular; y los actos de corrupción que involucran a elementos pertenecientes, al menos, a dos países. Como es lógico, para que dichas conductas puedan relacionarse con el concepto de corrupción administrativa es imprescindible que en las mismas intervenga algún sujeto representativo del Estado, o que de alguna forma se encuentre afectado el normal funciona miento de la administración pública de alguno de los Estados intervinientes, aun cuando la relación irregular se trabe con una empresa privada u organización no gubernamental de otro país.
(...)

7

IV. 2. Corrupción unipersonal o plurisubjetiva

En este marco de estudio referido a los distintos tipos de corrupción, cabe mencionar algunos que pueden resultar útiles a fin de llevar a cabo una adecuada descripción en cuanto al desarrollo de los esquemas de corrupción imperantes en la administración pública. ( )

El fenómeno de la corrupción también ha sido clasificado de acuerdo con la percepción que la opinión pública desarrolla respecto de ciertos actos irregulares. Bajo este parámetro se han identificado tres hipótesis diferentes que han sido de nominadas como corrupción: a) reprochable, b) ambigua y c) tolerable. En el primer caso, la sociedad en general expresa o hace evidente su consenso respecto a la necesidad de sancionar un determinado acto irregular; en el supuesto siguiente, en cambio, existe una opinión imprecisa o dudosa en punto a la aprobación o no de una especifica conducta ilícita; y final mente, pueden identificarse circunstancias en donde la mayor parte e de la opinión pública considera ciertos actos desviados como tolerables o permisibles, por lo que en consecuencia, no se percibe una exigencia de criminalización respecto de los mismos. Por supuesto, diversos serán los factores que influirán en el individuo para caracterizar una determinada conducta corrupta; dichos elementos tendrán que ver, por ejemplo, con el ámbito donde impacte el acto en cuestión, va sea, entre otros, económico, político, judicial, ele.; pero también, si las consecuencias del mismo se producen a corto o largo plazo, si se trata en ese caso de un acto incidental o, por el contrario, de un sistema estructural de corrupción, si afecta a altos funcionarios o empleados públicos de rango inferior, si el acto irregular involucra, o no, montos elevados de transacción, etcétera.(...)

IV. 5. Corrupción aislada y corrupción sistémica

(...) donde uno o varios actos de corrupción son ejecutados por un funcionario que actúa individualmente, o de manera acotada, sin que se verifiquen conexiones importantes con otros agentes para llevar a cabo dichas conductas, y la corrupción sistémica, la cual se produce cuando los mecanismos y las prácticas corruptas vigentes reemplazan de manera efectiva el entramado legal y organizativo de un determinado sector de la administración pública.

En aquellos ámbitos públicos donde se desarrolla un estado de corrupción sistémica, las irregularidades constituyen la norma mientras que los estándares de comportamientos exigibles a los funcionarios para que la administración pueda alcanzar sus objetivos de un modo regular y eficaz son la excepción. Aquí la conducta desviada se encuentra institucionalizada de tal manera que el castigo de acciones corruptas resulta infrecuente, siendo que en realidad se observa un ámbito de protección e impunidad respecto de los comportamientos indebidos.

IV. 6. Corrupción descendente o ascendente

A fin de profundizar las diferentes características que asume el funcionamiento de los sistemas de corrupción, es interesante destacar aquella tipología efectuada a partir del análisis de la estructura jerárquica en donde se originan los actos irregulares. Teniendo en consideración que la administración pública constituye una organización esquematizada a partir de rangos o grados, es posible distinguir aquellos sistemas de corrupción que se inician y desarrollan en los más altos niveles del organismo administrativo, y que se despliegan luego hacia los estratos más bajos: esquema identificado como corrupción descendente o corrupción arribaabajo; y los sistemas de corrupción que se originan en los niveles inferiores y que se dinamizan posteriormente en sentido ascendente en la jerarquía, los cuales pueden identificarse como corrupción ascendente o corrupción abajo-arriba."

Here is Ariel Todarello's classification of corruption:

1 – as to reach: national or transnational;
2 – as to the subject: sole or group;
3 – as to the gathering of people: isolated or systemic corruption;
4 – as to the hierarchy of deviations of functional conduct: upward or downward corruption.

Corruption has as many meanings as the faces of human evil, and it seems certain that where there is a dispute over power, it will be the driving force of those who justify ends by means, in the exercise of a utilitarianism that dishonors ethics, morals and law. This is also the perspective of Manuel Villoria Mendieta (2000: 25-27) when he points out in his course on administrative ethics:

> "La corrupción se puede definir desde diferentes perspectivas económica, jurídica, sociológica, no obstante, desde una perspectiva politológica, ha sido mayoritariamente definida con un fuerte componente valorativo, pues en general se refiere al incumplimiento de deberes derivados del ejercicio de cargo público y a un abuso de confianza. Las definiciones existentes se pueden integrar en cuatro grupos:
> En primer lugar, existen las definiciones vinculadas al abuso de cargo público o al incumplimiento de normas jurídicas por parte de los responsables públicos. Según Bayley (1989), corrupción es el abuso de autoridad por razones de beneficio particular no necesariamente monetario. En términos jurídicos comparativos, el cohecho suele ir vinculado a la presencia de un empleado público que tiene una intención corrupta, que recibe beneficios de la acción corrupta, cuyo acto oficial tiene relación directa con el valor conseguido, y cuando existe intención de influenciar o ser influenciado en el ejercicio de cargo público. En una visión general del fenómeno, corrupción seria toda acción tomada por un empleado público en el ejercicio de su cargo, que se desviara de las obligaciones jurídicamente establecidas para el mismo

por razones de interés privado, familiar, personal, con beneficios pecuniarios o de status. O cualquier violación de las normas contra el uso abusivo de cargo público en beneficio privado (Nye, 1989). Una lectura del Titulo XIX del vigente Código Penal español nos permitirá apreciar los diferentes tipos penales que la corrupción engloba: prevaricación, cohecho, infidelidad en la custodia de documentos, fraude, malversación de caudales públicos, abuso en el ejercicio de la función... Estas definiciones son demasiado estrechas y dejan fuera fenómenos dignos de estudio, fenómenos que aunque no entran en categorías jurídicamente penalizadas atentan contra la legitimidad de los regímenes políticos y pueden producir cambios sustanciales a medio o largo plazo en los mismos (Heidenheimer et al., 1989). No obstante, los estudios que el grupo de trabajo de la OCDE sobre el soborno en las transacciones económicas internacionales ha realizado, muestran que solo este tipo de corrupción mueve 23 billones de pesetas al año en el mundo, con precios muy variables que van desde el 30 por 100 en los contratos de armas al 5 por 100 en los contratos de infraestructuras, circunstancia que ha movido a la aprobación del primer Convenio de la OCDE de lucha contra la corrupción, el pasado mes de febrero de 1999.

Segundo, existen definiciones centradas en el mercado. Estas definiciones suelen usarse allí donde no existe un desarrollo jurídico suficientemente elevado como para poder categorizar adecuadamente todas las conductas corruptas. También son adecuadas para el análisis económico de la corrupción. Un funcionario corrupto seria aquel que utiliza su cargo como un negocio, un negocio cuya cuenta de resultados busca maximizar; el volumen de sus ingresos depende de la situación del mercado y de su talento para encontrar el punto de máxima ganancia en la curva de la demanda del público (Van Klaveren, 1989). Quizás estemos mas ante una explicación que ante una definición, en estos casos. Lo cierto es que se sustituyen los elementos valorativos y morales por la «maximización del beneficio» como criterio de definición. Tras estas definiciones suele encontrarse un cierto funcionalismo, pues vienen a reconocer que estos mecanismos de mercado cumplen una función social en determinadas sociedades. La crítica a esta opción es su propia tautología y la inmovilidad en la que sitúa el análisis y elaboración de políticas de cambio.

En tercer lugar, se podrían incluir las definiciones centradas en el interés general. Para Friedrich (1989), la corrupción existe cuando un responsable de un puesto público, con unas funciones y atribuciones definidas, es, por medios monetario o de otra naturaleza no legalmente prevista, inducid o a actuar favoreciendo a quien proporciona el beneficio y, por ello, dañando al público y a sus intereses. Esta definición podría incluir toda política pública o programa que se adopta o implanta considerando los intereses de solo una parte afectada, dados los beneficios que esta parte puede proporcionar a los empleados públicos responsables. O, incluso, toda acción tomada en el sentido de influir en una política pública con tal interés privado, sin perjuicio de los efectos sustanciales que tal acción pueda provocar. Con esta definición e abre un riquísimo debate sobre la actuación de los grupos de interés y sus conexiones con los empleados públicos de nivel superior. La influencia de los plutócratas sobre las decisiones y políticas públicas, cuando se hacen por interés puramente privado, vía financiación de partidos o contribuciones a campañas, quedarían incluidas dentro de este concepto de corrupción, aun cuando fuera legal tal actuación (Heidenheimer et al, 1989). Es evidente que toda la discusión sobre sistemas de financiación de partidos políticos queda muy influenciada por este concepto. También cobran otra dimensión las dificultades de ciertos políticos para aclarar de donde provienen fondos para sus campanas.

Finalmente, algunos autores critican las aproximaciones más moralistas e introducen una concepción histórica y sociológica, vinculada a la percepción social del fenómeno. Ciertamente, el entorno político, económico y social de ciertos países africanos es muy diferente del de Estados Unidos o el Reino Unido, con lo que la aplicación de los criterios domésticos anglosajones para analizar la corrupción en dichos países es totalmente inadecuada (Leys, 1989). El propio análisis histórico nos demuestra que conductas consideradas actualmente corruptas eran perfectamente validas en Europa Occidental varios siglos atrás; así Montesquieu defendía la venta de cargos públicos sobre otros métodos de nombramiento, defensa que también realizo Bentham, basándose en que permitía a los más ricos y de clase media - frente a la aristocracia - acceder a dichos cargos (Heidenheimer et al., 1989). Esta aproximación al fenómeno de la corrupción nos lleva a distinguir tres tipos de corrupción: negra, gris y blanca (Heidenheimer, 1989). La corrupción negra incluye todo el conjunto de acciones condenadas tanto por las elites morales del país correspondiente como por la ciudadanía en general; en ella suele existir una congruencia entre la ley y la opinión pública. La corrupción gris corresponde a aquella ambigua situación donde no hay consenso, pero donde sectores relevantes de la población - elite están a favor de la condena; puede ocurrir que existan normas que sancionen tal tipo de acciones y, sin embargo, la ciudadanía no rechace abiertamente tales conductas. Un ejemplo típico fue el producid o por la prohibición del consumo de alcohol en los Estados Unidos en los años 1920. O la defraudación a Hacienda en el pago de impuestos en determinados países sin elevada cultura cívica. La corrupción blanca está libre de oposición fuerte por parte del conjunto de la sociedad, ni la elite ni la ciudadanía en general la condenan abiertamente, por el contrario, la toleran, aunque no totalmente, si en alguno de sus aspectos; en este supuesto no existen leyes condenatorias de tales prácticas dada su falta de apoyo generalizado. El desarrollo moral de los individuos y de las sociedades, de acuerdo con la famosa tipología por etapas de Kohlberg (1984), permite explicar cómo lo que en un momento es considerado corrupción blanca pasa a

13

ser gris y, finalmente negra. Un ejemplo típico puede ser el tratamiento del tráfico de influencias en nuestro país. El problema con esta aproximación puede ser la falta de un punto de vista moral desde el que juzgar las conductas, con el correspondiente relativismo."

On the political aspect, Mendieta says that corruption refers to noncompliance with the duties derived from the exercise of public office and to the abuse of trust or authority due to personal benefits and not necessarily a monetary benefit.

There can be many interests, like nepotism, help to friends, help to religious or charitable associations, etc. In reality, personal interest overlaps with the collective for the corrupt.

In brief, Mendieta intends to integrate the existing definitions of corruption into four groups, which include:

1 - definitions that derive from the most diverse forms of exploitation of the position, job, function or term to achieve personal gain;

2 - definitions that focus on the market where there is no degree of legal development capable of typifying all corrupt conduct, adequate environment for corrupt officials to take advantage of such a gap to "negotiate" the political and administrative decisions to the argument that corruption is a means to maximize results;

3 - definitions centered on the interests of groups that finance or contribute to the campaigns of leaders who become hostages of their financiers and are forced to govern for the group they represent and not to serve the interests of the people; and

4 - definitions of a historical and sociological nature linked to the perception of the political, economic and social environment of corruption. Such definitions register a difference between the concept of what corruption is in Africa, the United States, and the United Kingdom, among others, and assert that historical analysis shows that conduct that was once considered corrupt is not nowadays. For example, as when Montesquieau and Jeremias Bentham advocated the sale of public offices and other types of appointments to the argument that the rich and the middle class would come to power and not just the aristocrats.

In fact, historically and sociologically, corruption can be relativized in time and space, for what was considered as corrupt conduct at one moment ceases to be in another, but it is nevertheless undeniable that the intrinsic concept of the term corruption has never lost its negative significance and relationship to a reprehensible conduct.

António Manuel Hespanha (2005: 237, 240), referring to the logical interpretation according to the aristotelian-scholastic dialectic, recalls that for such a school *"Therefore, defining consists in framing an initial idea in a system of logically hierarchical concepts"*, emphasizing that the search for conceptual truth also resides in the principle of authority, regardless of how critical it may be. Following is his analysis:

"The use of authority's argument is very characteristic of medieval legal thinking. Theoretically the value of this argument was based on the presumption that the invoked author was a profound connoisseur of that subject. (*doctor est peritus*/the doctor is an expert). However, his opinion was not mandatory, only valid until it was invalidated by a superior one. Thus, as long as there are no factors of decadence, the invocation of the authority argument and the *opinio comniu nis doctorum* (common opinion of the doctors) do not signify a rigid dogmatism for juridical science, as many people would think. It would suggest an open mentality in which it was important at all times to confront the points of view of the various authors because definitive truths were not recognized. It becomes clear how the invocation of the argument *ab auctoritate* is linked to the dialectical and not definitive nature of legal solutions. Since these always admitted discussion and were only probable, it was important to reinforce this probability by showing that the proposed solution was accepted by most authors. However, this probability would never become a certainty, even if one invoked thousands of opinions to corroborate it. ("The Doctors of Glory, and the same Rodoffredus, and many as they were, even if they said so, would all err." Cino da Pistóia, 14th century."

The criticism of Hespanha is based on the argument of authority, but its validity and usefulness extends to the present day, reason why we will use the "argument of authority" of justice, morality and law to conceptualize, relate causes, describe effects, identify allies, and propose solutions to fight corruption. Hespanha himself (2006: 242-243) in dissecting the argument of authority, emphasizes how virtuous it can be in clarifying obscure questions, as can be inferred from of the excerpt that we transcribe below:

> "(...) it is described by Gribaldo de Mopha (1541) in the following mnemonic: (1) Introduction to the analysis of the text, first literal interpretation; 2) division of the text into its logical parts, with the definition of the figure speech used and its logical concatenation, through dialectical notions of gender, species, and so on; 3) based on this logical ordering, systematic text editing; 4) articulation of parallel cases, of examples, of judicial precedents; 5) thorough reading of the text, i.e., reading of text in light of the logical and institutional context built in the previous stages; 6) indication of the nature of the institute (material cause), its distinctive characteristics (formal cause), its rationale (efficient cause), and its purposes (final cause); 7) further observations, an indication of general rules (brocards) and opinions of famous jurists (dicta); 8) objections to the proposed interpretation, denoting the dialectical nature of opinions on legal matters and contestations, with wide use of the Aristotelian-scholastic dialectic.

The preamble to the Universal Declaration of Human Rights (UN) fits us all as members of the human family in the following terms:

> "The General Assembly recognizes that the inherent dignity and the equal and inalienable rights of all members of the human family is the foundation of freedom, justice and peace in the world..."

Since the term corruption has the same negative connotation all over the world, it seems appropriate to regard the conscious and free conduct of the corrupt as an evil that affects all members of the human family, reason why we must fight against it, as we would a lethal enemy.

CHAPTER 2

The Perpetuation Of Corruption Through Time And Space

Evolution is a reality for the species of the planet, in a back-and-forth symbiosis in time and space.

Once the environment influenced man to the point of making him a nomad in search of subsistence, but over time man reversed logic, rationalized the environment, and entrapped it according to his purposes.

Charles de Lennay (1994: 94-95) studied the relation of man with the environment and asserted:

> "Si las especies se transforman según los cambios de su medio, este ultimo sufre transformaciones debidas a esas especies. La composición del aire que respiramos es el producto de la evolución de las plantas. En el inicio de la vida, los primeros seres vivos que han sido dotados de fotosíntesis, las cianobacterias (antiguamente llamadas algas azules) produjeron todo el oxígeno de la atmosfera, lo que transformo radicalmente sus propias condiciones de vida al mismo tiempo que las de las restantes especies."

In this evolutionary journey, we seek evidence of ethical-moral evolution of a man who can play the role of engineer, telematics specialist, economist, jurist, or scientist, yet sometimes is not able of small acts of solidarity.

At certain times in history, the image of man is of an extreme utilitarian, with a domesticated instinct and the latent evil within himself, wiling to subjugate the neighbor whenever power is at stake.

Whether the creationist man or the evolutionist one, subjugating is the rule, sharing is the exception and being honest is the rare quality to be praised.

Corruption is a phenomenon as old as mankind. It historically walks side by side with man throughout his journey, and despite the fact that time has proven that the phenomenon is an incurable cancer, it also leaves no doubt that it can be reduced to tolerable levels, as it is demonstrated by the educational process of some countries in which justice, morality, and law have become values that amalgamate a more dignified living in society.

If world leaders invest heavily in education, we can push the human species to the stages of development that ethics, morality and law preach and that today only fit in a hypothetical prism.

Ethics is learned. This is why we share with John Locke (2000: 45) the idea that in the field of knowledge there are no innate practical principles, especially in the field of justice and morality, since *"Justice and Truth are the common Ties of Society; and therefore, even Outlaws, and Robbers, who break with all the World besides, must keep Faith and Rules of Equity amongst themselves, or else they cannot hold together. But will anyone say, that those that live by Fraud and Rapine, have Innate Principles of Truth and Justice, which they allow and assent to?*

Human justice and morality always lack proof, which implies that they are not innate, they are part of the construction of the theory of cognoscence. Locke (2000: 46) states:

> "Moral rules need a proof, ergo not innate. Another reason that makes me doubt of any innate practical principles is, that I think there cannot any one moral rule be proposed whereof a man may not justly demand a reason."

History is prodigal in demonstrating that people follow a course of learning in which questioning increases the hope of producing a less formal and more substantial justice, gradually neutralizing the blind credulity so easy to be governed, as it also believes John Locke (2000: 53):

> "(...) And it was of no small advantage to those who affected to be masters and teachers, to make this

18

the principle of principles, - that principles must not he questioned. For, having once established this tenet, - that there are innate principles, it put their followers upon a necessity of receiving some doctrines as such; which was to take them off from the use of their own reason and judgment, and put them on believing and taking them upon trust without further examination: in which posture of blind credulity, they might be more easily governed by, and made useful to some sort of men, who had the skill and office to principle and guide them. Nor is it a small power it gives one man over another, to have the authority to be the dictator of principles, and teacher of unquestionable truths; and to make a man swallow that for an innate principle which may serve to his purpose who teacheth them. Whereas had they examined the ways whereby men came to the knowledge of many universal truths, they would have found them to result in the minds of men from the being of things themselves, when duly considered; and that they were discovered by the application of those faculties that were fitted by nature to receive and judge of them, when duly employed about them."

In order to better understand our past and to correct the course of learning history about the multiple forms of corruption and its struggle, one should always question his own truths, including being an example of overcoming for future generations, since history has proven our corruptible nature.

2.1 – Corruption in Celestial Paradise (a Judaic-Christian Conception)

Professor Roberto Romano, Chair of the Department of Philosophy and Ethics at the University of Campinas, São Paulo, commenting on the phenomenon of corruption, its distribution and attempts to control it among the three branches of the Brazilian government said: *The only place where there is no corruption is in paradise!*

It is common among Christians (whether millennial or not) to say that

Lucifer served God in heaven until the day he resolved to rebel. In this enterprise, he dragged with him a third part of the angels who, in the end, were driven away from heavenly heaven by God.

Here are some biblical texts used to corroborate this thesis:

"How art thou fallen from heaven, O Lucifer, son of the morning! How art thou cut down to the ground, which didst weaken the nations!" (Isaiah 14:12)

(…)

"For some are already turned aside after Satan." (1 Timothy 5:15)

(...)

"I know thy works, and where thou dwellest, even where Satan's seat is: and thou holdest fast my name, and hast not denied my faith, even in those days wherein Antipas was my faithful martyr, who was slain among you, where Satan dwelleth." (Revelation 2:13)

Note that in the passages above Satan is treated with great and loving distinction, for he is called *son of the morning, Lucifer.*

If the thesis that Lucifer, the angel of light, has rebelled and has gathered innumerable other angels as preached in Christianity is true, there is no reason to deny the existence of corruption in heavenly paradise, and less that it was God himself who created hell to keep the devil in there, even though he failed in that purpose, says Philip G. Zimbardo, a Professor at Stanford University, Psychology Nobel Prize in 2003.

The question is: if God created hell as a place of suffering to throw the devil into because of his corruption, why do we keep our corrupt in the paradise of impunity?

2.2 – Corruption in Earthly Paradise (a Judaic-Christian Conception)

Creationist theory recognizes the existence of corruption also in the Garden of Eden, the earthly paradise.

Note that the biblical account evokes the following acts and facts:

1 - the legislator: God;

2- the law as a prohibitive order in regard to eating the fruit of the tree of the knowledge of good and evil;

3 - the active corruptor: the serpent;

4 - the passive corrupts: Adam and Eve;

5 - sin: conscious and free conduct of the deviation or breaking of the covenant;

6 - the punishment: having to work the land for its own sustenance, childbirth pains, and, in the case of the serpent, that seemed to walk, God imposed the curse of having to crawl.

Whether in the heavenly paradise or in the earthly paradise, it takes two to tango. Here is the biblical account of corruption in the earthly paradise:

> "Genesis 3 - Now the serpent was craftier than any of the wild animals the Lord God had made. He said to the woman, "Did God really say, 'You must not eat from any tree in the garden'?" (...)Then the Lord God said to the woman, "What is this you have done?" The woman said, "The serpent deceived me, and I ate."
>
> So the Lord God said to the serpent, "Because you have done this, Cursed are you above all livestock and all wild animals! You will crawl on your belly and you will eat dust all the days of your life. (...)To the woman he said, "I will make your pains in childbearing very severe; with painful labor you will give birth to children. Your desire will be for your husband, and he will rule over you."
>
> To Adam he said, "Because you listened to your wife and ate fruit from the tree about which I commanded you, 'You must not eat from it,' "Cursed is the ground because of you; through painful toil you will eat food from it all the days of your life." (Underlined by the author)

There are many examples of corruption in the Bible: greed, avarice, envy, betrayal, crimes of passion. For each of these conducts we can find several passages, such as the following:

1 - Homicide caused by envy / turpitude

> "And these words of Esau, her elder son, were told to Rebekah: and she sent and called Jacob her younger son, and said unto him, Behold, thy brother Esau, as touching thee, doth comfort himself, purposing to kill thee." (Genesis 27:42)

2 - Avarice and love of money

> "For the love of money is the root of all evil: which while some coveted after, they have erred from the faith, and pierced themselves through with many sorrows." (1 Timothy 6:10)

3 - The greed of the shepherds over the flock

> "Yea, they are greedy dogs which can never have enough, and they are shepherds that cannot understand: they all look to their own way, every one for his gain, from his quarter." (Isaiah 56:11)

4 - Betrayal

> "After two days was the feast of the Passover, and of unleavened bread: and the chief priests and the scribes sought how they might take him by craft, and put him to death." (Mark 14:1)

Both in the old and the new testaments man carries an original sin that makes him a corrupt being waiting for salvation, waiting for the "Lamb of God that taketh away the sin of the world."

Quentin Skinner (1996: 287) analyzing the principles of Lutheranism, which separated Church from State and the attack on the proclaimed humanistic virtues, says:

"The true situation, as Luther seeks to indicate in the title of his tract, is that our wills remain at all times in total bondage to sin. We are all so 'corrupt and averse from God' that we have no hope of ever being able to will 'things which please God or which God wills' (pp.175-6). All our actions proceed from our 'averse and evil' natures, which are completely enslaved to Satan, and thus ensure that we can 'do nothing but averse and evil things' (pp.98, 176). The result is that 'through the one transgression of the one man, Adam, we are all under sin and damnation', and are left with 'no capacity to do anything but sin and be damned' (p.272)."

Thus, man (another creation of God who would give him as much trouble as Lucifer did) was created to live among the two greatest spiritual forces, God and the devil.

Free will imposed itself and by accepting the offer of the "serpent" freely and consciously the human eyes opened to the knowledge of good and evil. Henceforth, his life became an eternal struggle to resist the devil and to please God, whom he, in theory, would like to serve.

Believing in this course of history and adding to it the divine attributes of omnipresence, omniscience and omnipotence, a plausible interpretation is that the Creator already knew all the chaos that his creations would bring. In other words, God created the angels and men knowing that they would fall into the abyss of temptation and yet he hung them in an unlocked cage above this abyss.

2.3 – Corruption under the Light of the Theory of Evolution

The Evolutionary Theory coincides with the Creationist in the belief of a war in nature, with the subtle difference that for creationism war is in "human nature" and for evolutionism war lies in the environment of which man is part.

What matters is that we perceive that in either conception the strongest, or the most astute wins, as Charles Robert Darwin (2006: 80; 116-117; 154) states:

"Si el hombre puede producir, y seguramente ha producido, resultados grandes con sus modos metódicos o inconscientes de selección, ¿qué no podrá efectuar la selección natural? El hombre puede obrar sólo sobre caracteres externos y visibles. La Naturaleza - si se me permite personificar la conservación o supervivencia natural de los más adecuados - no atiende a nada por las apariencias, excepto en la medida que son útiles a los seres."

(...)

"La selección natural obra exclusivamente mediante la conservación y acumulación de variaciones que sean provechosas, en las condiciones orgánicas e inorgánicas a que cada ser viviente está sometido en todos los periodos de su vida. El resultado final es que todo ser tiende a perfeccionarse más y más, en relación con las condiciones. Este perfeccionamiento conduce inevitablemente al progreso gradual de la organización del mayor número de seres vivientes, en todo el mundo. Pero aquí entramos en un asunto complicadísimo, pues los naturalistas no han definido, a satisfacción de todos, lo que se entiende por progreso en la organización."

(...)

"Así, la cosa más elevada que somos capaces de concebir, o sea la producción de los animales superiores, resulta directamente de la guerra de la naturaleza, del hambre y de la muerte. Hay grandeza en esta concepción de que la vida, con sus diferentes fuerzas, ha sido alentada por el Creador en un corto número de formas o en una sola, y que, mientras este planeta ha ido girando según la constante ley de la gravitación, se han desarrollado y se están desarrollando, a partir de un principio tan sencillo, infinidad de formas bellísimas y maravillosas."

Thus, it is undeniable that corruption began in the heavenly paradise and "descended" into the earthly paradise, contaminating both the sinful creationist man and the fragile evolutionist man, for in Darwin the most striking thing to conceive is that the creation of superior animals results directly from the war in nature, from the war arising from hunger and death.

When he refers to the force of nature, Darwin devises that if man can produce such great results with his methodical and unconscious modes of selection, let alone nature that to nothing and no one attends to appearance, but to what is useful to the evolution of beings. For Darwin there is a natural war for survival and the extinction of the weakest is no reason to regret because this is the natural law of evolution.

2.4 — Corruption from a Theological Perspective

Theology is the study of God. In fact, after I dropped out of my bachelor's degree in Theology by the Baptist Theological Faculty of Brasília in the second year, I ended up thinking that theology is the study of God's domination over any and all creation, because there is no man without God nor God without man and what permeates this relation between creator and creature is the power that one has over the other.

When we look at creationist theory, we learn that the history of man's creation is narrated in two chapters, and the rest is an account of his temptation, fall, murder, and every kind of sordid sin a human is capable of committing. We all know that the counting of that time when everything was created does not obey the Julian or Gregorian calendars.

In the light of the theory of knowledge it seems possible to say that creationism is based on the "Supreme Good" and on its greater human creature (man) condemned by disobedience (sin).

Sin for theology means to miss the mark, to disobey the Supreme Lawgiver, creator of good and evil. Notice the initial relationship between the principles of authority and hierarchy, and also the connection between disobedience and punishment as a relation of cause and effect.

The theory of *conditio sine qua non*, before being appropriated by law, resided in theology. After all, the initial corruption of mankind had as its cause a commissive act, conscious and free conduct of the disobedient man who chose to know good and evil, the result of which was divine sanction, because of the imbalance in the relation of forces between creator and creature, between those who dominate and those who are dominated.

For theology it matters little to know about God and much about his power, because his is what gives light to the idea of a sinful man and eternally guilty by the original disobedience that unleashed the chaos.

This conception of sin as a cause worthy of a sanctioning result will be perfected over time by the Church and later excised by the State.

Historical man follows his course laden with inferiority complexes imposed by religion and the State.

Inspired by the idea of sin as a conduit for imbalances, Emilio A. Albistur (1996: 531) describes corruption as a social sin that produces other social sins. The author says:

> "Surge una pregunta: ¿Por qué querer calificar a la corrupción como pecado social y generadora de estructuras de pecado? Es decir, ¿por qué dar prioridad uno al tema moral? Son varias las razones: el binomio corrupción-injusticia es inseparable. Juan Pablo II dijo: 'se puede hablar ciertamente de «egoísmo» y de «estrechez de miras». Se puede hablar también de «cálculos políticos errados» y de «decisiones económicas imprudentes». Y en cada una de estas calificaciones se percibe una resonancia de carácter ético-moral' (SRS, ns 36)."

If for creationism evil is in man a kind of "original sin," in opposition to the anarchism of Mikhail Aleksandrovitch Bakunin and later that of Leon Tolstoy assures that the State as well as property would be the source of all evil and not man.

Nelson Lehmann (1985: 91) states that:

> "For anarchists evil lies outside of man. Contrary to skeptical Christian realism, they usually reveal a naive revolutionary optimism, certain that the removal of the external source of evils will free mankind to enjoy the paradise inherent in its own nature."

2.5 — Corruption from a Sociological Perspective

It is impossible to conceive of sociology without the social-historical conditions of man in his environment. This social living is a relationship that affects everyone, whether in thinking, feeling, or wanting.

Anna Maria de Castro and Edmundo F. Dias in introducing the sociological thinking of Durkheim, Weber, Marx and Parsons say that:

> "Any analysis of the conduct of society or of the human destiny collides with the 'absolute', 'intangible', and 'sacred' character of culturally recognized values and social institutions." (Introduction to sociological thinking – Eldorado – 4th edition, page 22)

Karl Mannheim, in the construction of his sociology of ideology and utopia says with irreproachable property:

> "we belong to a group not only because we are born in it, not only because we confess to belonging to it, and, lastly, not because we offer it our loyalty and fidelity, but mainly because we see the world and certain things in the world the way this group sees them." (Introduction to sociological thinking – Eldorado – 4th edition, page 28)

Maria Stela Grossi Porto and Tom Dwyer (2006, pp. 89-90), analyzing ethics in the social man, creator and interpreter of values that orbit around the must-be or not, starts from an ontological idea when says that the free man is the one who can opt for the ends; that this rational and free man will have to grasp the various options or means to be used until the desired ends are attained, and that, in order to decide, he needs criteria or values. Here is an excerpt surely deserves transcription:

> "The problem with Jonah's argumentation is as simple as: how to extrapolate the altruism that exists in family relations to society and, even more difficult, to all mankind? Jonah formulates the first imperative of his ethics not answering clearly as he says: The first ethical imperative is that mankind be! Therefore, it precedes the first principle of the ethics of responsibility itself. The imperative of the obligation to be and continue to be (in the future) does not derive from a doctrine of acting, but, as Jonas notes, (...) from metaphysics as a doctrine of Being, from which the idea of man is part "(JONAS, 1984, p.92).

27

Jonas's argument that follows anticipates the reader's objections: "This goes against the strongest dogmas of our time: first that there are no metaphysical truths, and second, that a duty is not deduced from Being." (JONAS, 1984, p.92).

At least the author sets forth the facts: the metaphysics contained in all ethics and also in those that fight metaphysics with "materialist" ideas also appears in the ethics of responsibility. Jonah asserts that he openly takes on the metaphysical foundation of duty (Jonas 1984: 93). The concept of must-be comes from an ontological idea; as an idea, though, it is still a metaphysical concept.

Should man be? To answer this question Jonas expands the problem and asks: what is preferable, Being or Not Being? Classifying it as prior to Leibniz's problematic ("why is it something rather than nothing?"), he states that his question focuses on "value." If we could identify Being as value at this elementary level, we would undoubtedly have a more solid basis for reflecting on "values" within society.

Before Jonah returns to the question of value, a sine qua non concept of any ethics, he makes a lengthy examination of the "end," or rather the purposes in nature. The meaning of this excursion is to show that in nature there are processes guided by a causality of purpose (Ziel kausalitat). To be able to define ends is not, then, exclusively, an attribute of the human subject of being able to define ends. The very generation of life on Earth would be one of those purposes contained or generated by nature. This, in turn, is not only organic nature, the inorganic Being itself seems to know ends, it manages to order physical processes to take an evolutionary direction. Understanding man as an end of nature, there arises, curiously, an end that can choose ends. Usually, the one who may opt is called a "free" person. With "freedom" comes the need for discernment among various options. In order to decide whether we need criteria or values; we also need an ethic.

(...)

> The Being wants to be. And life wants to live. We feel this by contemplating the purposes in nature. Ethics is necessary because of the choices that man, as an actor, has, since he has the freedom to be able to act against the ends of life. Do what then? Live and act responsibly, taking into account the future and distant consequences of our actions. We can never risk everything, we can never risk the conditions of life on Earth. Caution thus becomes the highest ethical prescription."

In his inaugural address to the Social Sciences Course at Bourdeaux in 1887, Émile Durkheim in Introduction to Sociological Thinking - Eldorado - 4th edition - p. 49, stated that:

> "Societies are what we make of them, there is no reason why we should ask ourselves what they are, but what we should make of them. Since we cannot count on its nature, it is not necessary to know it; it is enough to set the end that they must fulfill and find the best way for this purpose to be met. For example, we will state that the purpose of society is to assure each individual the exercise of their rights, and from this we deduce all sociology."

Sociology as a science that studies the social man in his historical path and the social facts he produces is not blind to see that this man who thinks, feels, and wants makes dubious ethical choices capable of endangering the whole, regardless of how much the parts that compose it are different from the "whole" proclaimed or agreed upon.

The action of an individual or of a political party, for example, is not and cannot be considered as the whole, although it influences its composition. For instance, by seeing the social body as the "social whole", every act or manifestation of will performed can influence the conception and composition of the whole, to the point of denaturalizing it.

In the event that this act is an act of corruption, if uncontrolled, it may alter the ethical and moral nature agreed upon for the social body. At this stage, either it is accepted that the social body will no longer be the same because it was denaturalized, or one fights the conduct to preserve the system agreed as the best for social body survival.

Skinner (1996: 184-185), talking about the analysis that Machiavelli did in the 16th century on corruption throughout history and what the subject mattered to the princes of his time says:

> "Machiavelli is the author who provides, without a doubt, the richest analysis of this theme. In a certain way, this concept is at the heart of the Discourses, because Machiavelli tells us that his main objective in this work is to advise "those princes and republics who wish to remain immune to corruption" … clarifying then that, when speaking about corruption, one understands, first and foremost, the inability of someone to dedicate his energies to the common good and - in parallel - the tendency to put his own interests above those of the community."

Therefore, for Machiavelli corruption is:

> "the inability of someone to dedicate his energies to the common good and - in parallel - the tendency to put his own interests above those of the community."

If ignorance of history can make us repeat our mistakes, our politicians and public officials seem to have failed this subject and seem to know Machiavelli only through the advice to use force necessary to maintain tyranny.

Historically there seems to be no doubt that corruption accompanies man far beyond his creeds, origins, ethnicity, or culture, as we will continue to prove.

2.6 — On the Existence and Antiquity of Corruption - in the Society of Men

Establishing a temporal framework in ancient times is not prudent, but there are historical facts whose source and landmark can be cited, such as the Code of Hammurabi written around the year 1700 BC in which we can find "fingerprints" of corruption. Here is an excerpt from Chapter I:

> "5. If a judge try a case, reach a decision, and present his judgment in writing; if later error shall appear in his decision, and it be through his own fault, then he shall pay twelve times the fine set by him in the case, and he shall be publicly removed from the judge's bench, and never again shall he sit there to render judgments."

Todarello (2008: 14, 18-19) pointed out that Socrates and his disciples in the 5th century BC perceived the corrosion caused by corruption in Greek democracy:

> "En su obra Las leyes, Platón construye determinadas observaciones que se encuentran relacionadas en forma directa con aquel fenómeno identificado actualmente como corrupción administrativa. Así, afirma: "Todo el que distraiga los caudales públicos, sea en mucha o en poca cantidad, debe ser castigado con una misma pena, porque la poca cantidad prueba en el que la distrae, no menos codicia, y sí menos poder". Dichos conceptos nos advierten acerca de la relevancia que el ateniense asignaba al cuidado y preservación del patrimonio público, como así también en cuanto a la identificación a su criterio de la "codicia" como impulso motivador de aquellos actos desviados que son desplegados por las personas que detentan el poder y que constituyen, en definitiva, el fenómeno de corrupción administrativa.
>
> (...)
>
> Refiriéndose luego expresamente al desarrollo impune de la conducta corrupta de los gobernantes, explica Trasímaco que "cuando un gobernante se ha apoderado de los bienes de sus ciudadanos y hasta de sus personas, reduciéndolos a la esclavitud, en vez de esos nombres injuriosos suele llamársele hombre feliz, hombre privilegiado, no solamente por los ciudadanos, sino hasta por aquellos que saben que no ha habido injusticia que no

haya consumado. Porque lo que reprochan la injusticia no lo hacen por miedo de cometerla, sino por temor a sufrirla". En definitiva, Trasímaco concluye que la injusticia es más ventajosa que la justicia: "De tal modo la injusticia, Sócrates, llevada hasta cierto punto, es más fuerte, más libre, más poderosa que la justicia".

A partir de ello, Sócrates se ubica en la posición contraria: "Por lo que a mí respecta, declaro que no estoy convencido y que no acepto que la injusticia sea más ventajosa que la justicia". Esgrime entonces que ningún gobierno honesto y no corrupto "procura su propio provecho, sino que, coma antes decíamos, procura y ordena en beneficio del gobernado, que es el más débil, y no en el interés del más fuerte... porque aquel que desea ejercer convenientemente su arte no ejecuta y no ordena nunca... lo que es más ventajoso para sí, sino para aquel para quien ejecuta y ordena'.' Luego agrega: "el verdadero gobernante no tiene de ningún modo en mira su propio interés sino el de los gobernados a quienes sirve". Sin duda, debe subrayarse la manera en que Platón, ya en aquel momento, elaboraba y enseñaba - a partir de una hipotética conversación - uno de los principios rectores del Estado de derecho, como es aquel referido a la búsqueda y persecución del bien común o general por parte de los agentes que componen el Estado; censurando de tal forma la comisión de aquellas acciones irregulares que persiguen la satisfacción de intereses personales a partir de la utilización de elementos gubernamentales provistos por una determinada situación de poder."

In the transcribed text we see an ethical Plato state that anyone who diverts public resources in small or large quantities should be punished with the same penalty because the deviation of little amounts shows no less greed, only less power.

Rich and accessible historical records on the empires of ancient civilizations demonstrate that the more power a public agent was delegated, the larger the frontiers of his corrupt acts and his vanity.

So it was with pharaohs, caesars, czars and it continues to be true with the ones who are able to use the appropriate circumstances for their purposes, such as Stalin, Hitler, Mussolini, Idi Amin Dada, and so many other right-wing and left-wing dictators that used power to their personal advantage, the advantage of their children and friends.

Claudio Fermin (2004: 41) states that "El culto a la personalidad se convierte en el hilo temático de los supuestos revolucionarios." The cult of personality is one of the cornerstones of corruption.

In Rome, between 106 and 43 BC, Marcus Tullius Cicero distilled his anger against the exploiters of the people, against those who treated public office as a source of personal satisfaction rather than using it as a tool to carve the "common well-being".

The dialogue translated by Janet Taylor Caldwell (1965: 464) between Cicero and the dictator Crassus is enlightening:

> "- I hope, noble Cicero," said Crassus in his rough but compelling voice. "that you are enjoying my poor dinner."
>
> "I am not accustomed to dinning so humbly," said Marcus.
>
> Julius, hearing this, laughed and nudged his host.
>
> (...)
>
> Crassus considered him from under his thick black brows. "I should like to see all men in Rome live thus. Do they not deserve the fruits of their labor? Alas, they are deprived of their rights, their honest luxuries. Do not all Romans deserve chariots and cars and fine horses and splendid houses? Who denies them?"
>
> "The government, no doubt," said Marcus. "The privileged. The greedy. The avaricious. The exploiters of the people."

I do not wish to sacralize the figure of the State as Cicero did because I agree with Friedrich Engels (vol.2: 181) when he states that the State is the fruit of the rationalization of the human inability to live in harmony:

> "The State is, therefore, by no means a power forced on society from without; just as little is it 'the reality of the ethical idea', 'the image and reality of reason', as Hegel maintains. Rather, it is a product of society at a certain

stage of development; it is the admission that this society has become entangled in an insoluble contradiction with itself, that it has split into irreconcilable antagonisms which it is powerless to dispel. But in order that these antagonisms, these classes with conflicting economic interests, might not consume themselves and society in fruitless struggle, it became necessary to have a power, seemingly standing above society, that would alleviate the conflict and keep it within the bounds of 'order'; and this power, arisen out of society but placing itself above it, and alienating itself more and more from it, is the State."

Moreover, the creation of the State in the ways we know it not only exposed our inability to live in harmony, but also gave rise to new classes of dangers arising from its institutional activities, as Nicolás Garcia Rivas (2006: 222) mentions:

"En el documento titulado Ciencia, sociedad y ciudadanos en Europa, la Comisión de la Unión Europea afirma que mientras las sociedades del pasado vivían bajo la permanente amenaza del peligro natural, gran parte de los riesgos a los que están expuestas las sociedades actuales tiene su origen en la propia actividad humana."

The emergence of the State also pluralized ethics and imposed State morality through the positivization of law, which, in the end, greatly accelerated the process of creating servants and masters, such as Victor Méndez Baiges (1997:123) when pondering Adam Smith's thoughts:

"La sociedad civilizada se caracteriza entonces, según Smith, porque tiene un gobierno y porque hay en ella desigualdad de clases, pero también porque hay mucha división del trabajo. Esto último explica que no solo haya en ella más riqueza, sino incluso que esta se desparrame sobre todos sus miembros, de forma que un industrioso campesino ingles vive mejor que un rey africano, dueño y señor de las vidas y haciendas de diez mil salvajes desnudos."

Civilized society thought of the State as the ideal form of association, and corrupt man saw in this association his best personal fulfillment.

The State sublimated the struggle for power and engendered both rational and irrational utilitarianism capable of justifying ends by means.

Reflecting on the relationship between the common good and corruption, Carlos Manfroni (1998: 19-20) says that this relationship is the exercise of power always in favor of rulers and that in classical Greek thinking, especially in Aristotle, corruption is the dividing line between the pure forms and the deviant forms of government. Here is an excerpt worth reflecting on:

> "La corrupción es un mal al que parecen haber estado expuestos los gobiernos en todos los tiempos y que consiste en el ejercicio del poder en provecho del gobernante, con desatención del bien común. La corrupción, en el pensamiento de los griegos clásicos y, muy particularmente, en el de Aristóteles, es la línea divisoria entre las formas de gobierno puras y las desviadas: "Cuando el dueño único, o la minoría, o la mayoría, gobiernan consultando el interés general, la constitución es pura necesariamente; cuando gobiernan en su propio interés, sea el de uno solo, sea el de la minoría, sea el de la multitud, la constitución se desvía del camino trazado por su fin, puesto que, una de dos cosas, o los miembros de la asociación no son verdaderamente ciudadanos o lo son, y en este caso deben tener su parte en el provecho común.
>
> Actualmente, ya casi en ningún país se discute la igualdad jurídica de los ciudadanos y, sin embargo, no todos tienen "su parte en el provecho común". Y al decir "su parte en el provecho común" no nos referimos a una división demagógica de los bienes sociales, sino a los beneficios que cualquier ciudadano puede esperar del Estado en un régimen capitalista: seguridad, atención de la salud, justicia, facilidades para la educación, información, regulación de las condiciones mínimas de trabajo, etcétera.
>
> Sin embargo, en un sentido, la corrupción no posee hoy la misma extensión que la que podía alcanzar en la Antigüedad. Precisamente, el mayor reconocimiento de

la igualdad jurídica de los ciudadanos y; la difusión de las comunicaciones han reducido las posibilidades del gobernante de obtener beneficios personales mediante el uso directo de la fuerza pública, sobre todo en Occidente. La corrupción requiere hoy cierto consenso; consenso viciado, impuro, pero consenso al fin. El soborno es la forma más común de ese consenso, aunque debe reconocerse que las dos partes – quien soborna y quien es sobornado – no tienen el mismo grado de libertad para elegir."

Manfroni says that corruption affected all the rulers of past and present days. In particular, we believe that even the rulers who are yet to come will surrender to it. Reason why what is intended with this work is not to propose the extinction of corruption, but to expose its innards so that we can know it and fight it effectively.

There will always be corruption where men are. There is no reason to think that hegemonic countries are free from it or that corruption is the cultural heritage of one or other people. In the US, e.g., The Almanac of Political Corruption, Scandals & Dirty Politics (2007: 4,184,263,292) makes sequential historical records that deserve citation. Here are some excerpts:

"Before 1776 - The United States created a demonstrably unique form of government after its independence from England, but it can't take credit for the concept of political corruption and scandal. British officials who were appointed to positions in the American colonies committed misdeeds from graft to bribery to extortion. One estimate of the loss to the British Treasury in the year 1765 due to corrupt colonial officials was £700,000 ($132 million in today's dollars). ( )

1940-1959

World War II did not so much diminish political corruption and scandal as divert it from the public eye. One of the few politicians active in uncovering political misdeeds during this period of national unity was Harry

Truman. Roosevelt's vice president Dogged and ruthless, Truman used congressional investigations to uncover fraud, waste, mismanagement, profiteering, and other irregular activity.(...)

On January 22, 1987, R. Budd Dwyer (1939-1987), Pennsylvania state treasurer, shot and killed himself during a televised news conference. Dwyer's troubles began in 1984 when he was implicated—but not charged—in a case that involved a no-bid award for a State contract. In 1986, Dwyer and a former chairman of the state Republican Party were indicted in a statewide bribery case that was tied to this previous investigation. On December 19, 1986, both men were convicted of bribery after a federal trial. Both declared their innocence, and there were reports that Dwyer had been offered a plea bargain, but had turned it down in anticipation of a favorable verdict. He killed himself a few. (...)

In the early years of the new century, the mayor of a New Jersey city was sent to prison; a U.S. congressman was censured for campaign finance violations; another congressman was convicted of fraud and racketeering; the lieutenant governor of Kentucky was sued by the government for Medicare fraud; the former state attorney general in Texas was indicted by a federal grand Jury; and Karl Rove, President George W. Bush's adviser, was scrutinized for his role in the publication of the name of an undercover CIA agent, the wife of an outspoken critic of the administration. And more. Is the situation getting better, or worse? Are politicians more scandal-prone and corrupt, or are we just paying more attention to their problems? Changes that have made an impact include mom laws governing campaign activity and donations, tougher regulations for interactions with lobbyists and constituents, and the narrowing of the concept of ethical practices. At the same time, more eyes keep watch over political activity, from citizens' groups to bloggers to scoop-coveting media outlets. Law-enforcement agencies, particularly the FBI, are also watching more closely and acting more aggressively, in a single recent year, according to a spokesperson for the FBI, the agency was involved in 2,200 corruption cases involving public officials, resulting in 800 convictions. The politicians are not likely becoming more corrupt, it's just becoming more likely that their corruption will be noticed."

In summary, it is estimated that the losses of the British treasury with acts of corruption practiced by colonial authorities, solely in the year 1765, correspond to US$ 132 million in today's numbers.

With rare exceptions, corruption in European countries is also astonishing, as Víctor Manuel Monti (1999: 58) observes:

"Otro autor que coincide en cuanto a que la expresión que nos ocupa ha tenido cambios en el ámbito sobre el que abarca su significado, es Eduardo Posada Carbó. Este sostiene la idea que «...la corrupción no es un fenómeno novedoso. Su presencia es tan antigua como la prostitución. O el contrabando. No obstante, con el correr del tiempo, la expresión ha tendido a variar de significado. El historiador Jean Claude Waquet ha mostrado como, para nuestros antepasados, la corrupción abarcaba un campo más amplio: la totalidad de la vida moral del ser humano. Era sinónimo de pecado. Y podía oscurecer la imagen de toda una época, como cuando Boais tuau, en su Teatro del mundo, en 1560, se refirió a un siglo como el nuestro tan corrupto, tan depravado y lleno de toda clase de vicios y abominaciones. Hoy el termino ha adquirid o un sentido más técnico, para señalar los malos manejos de los funcionarios públicos y su apropiación indebida de los recursos del estado."

If the young people learn from the elder, it is not surprising that Europe is the cradle of Latin American corruption. Cincunegui (1996; 169-170) says:

"La corrupción en países del G-7 como Italia y España es asombrosa en cuanto a sus dimensiones, y no solo en la actualidad, sino que ha sido permanente y continua a lo largo de gobiernos pertenecientes a partidos que a pesar de los escándalos han permanecido en el poder.

(...)

No en vano se han producido películas como 'Confesión de un Condenado a un Juez de Instrucción', 'El Enemigo Público Nro. 1', 'Un pequeño, pequeño burgués', entre otras, en las cuales se han dado muestras del accionar 'mafioso', sobretodo en la industria de la construcción publica y otras contrataciones del Estado.

Para Ferrajoli, el caso Berlusconi tiene visos de un tipo de corrupción que trae serios peligros para la democracia, sobre la base de técnicas mas mediáticas de captación de consenso, la confusión entre esfera pública y privada, la idea del carácter ilimitado del poder mayoritario y del poder de mercado."

To study a human phenomenon is to study man himself. The facts he produces are largely conditioned by his culture, which consequently influences his way of thinking and acting. Manuel Villoria Mendieta (2000: 87) points out:

"En general, la 'cultura es el componente subjetivo del equipamiento del que dispone una sociedad para enfrentarse a su entorno: los valores, las actitudes, las creencias, las técnicas y el conocimiento de su gente. Los factores políticos, económicos y otros factores externos tienen la misma importancia, pero no son determinantes por sí mismos ( ) lo que pasa en la mente de las personas es tan importante como lo que sucede fuera' (Inglehart, 1998, p. 72). Por ello, 'podemos afirmar que: 1. Las respuestas de las personas a sus situaciones se forman de acuerdo con sus orientaciones subjetivas, que varían entre las diferentes culturas y subculturas. 2. Estas variaciones en las orientaciones subjetivas reflejan las diferencias entre las experiencias de socialización de las personas, donde el aprendizaje temprano condiciona el aprendizaje posterior, haciendo el primero más difícil de anular.' (Inglehart,

1998, p. 23). Los ciudadanos y, con ellos, los empleados públicos son claramente influidos en su comportamiento por la cultura en la que viven y han sido socializados."

Keep in mind, though, that culture has not polarized between the public and the private. Mendieta (2000:88) suggests that it has become more and more popular in the most diverse fields of cognoscence and has become the generating or influential uterus of the social, political, legal, and economic man:

"La cultura política se puede transcribir mediante la descripción de las actitudes de los ciudadanos hacia los tres niveles del sistema político: el sistema, el proceso y las políticas (Almond et al., 1996, p. 44). Los estudios sobre cultura política en los tres niveles, indican, en general, rasgos de cultura cívica cuando se observa que existe: consenso sustancial sobre la legitimidad de las instituciones políticas y la dirección y contenido de las políticas públicas, una tolerancia general hacia la pluralidad de intereses y creencia en su reconciliabilidad y una sensación general de confianza en las aptitudes políticas de los ciudadanos y la confianza mutua (Almond 1998)."

We believe that with globalization spreading in all fields of social life, national culture is no longer the only determinant in the study of corruption. People from all continents are all hosts of this lethal virus that ruthlessly infects the private and public sector policies and rottens the social tissue, turning the democratic state of law into a source of empty promises.

The State has become the guardian of man and he can and must defend the social dignity he has been promised since only a strong State in the principles of freedom, equality, and solidarity can lead us to a substantial democracy.

On the importance of a State that catalyses society, which is a driver of social, political, and economic development, and is concerned with building a society to which institutions serve them, Mendieta (2000: 89) asserts:

"reivindicar un Estado fuerte - lo cual no implica un Estado grande ni omnipresente - con una sociedad civil fuerte. Sólo un Estado fuerte puede reforzar los mecanismos de socialización democráticos. Un Estado fuerte es el único capaz de negociar y dotar de eficacia hacia el interior las regulaciones y acuerdos transnacionales; además de asegurar en su interior el imperio de la Ley que reduzca los costos de transacción y facilite los intercambios. Pero, sobre todo, el Estado de la era de la globalización debe ser ese organismo intermedio entre las sociedades nacionales y el gran mercado global que proteja a sus comunidades frente a la mundialización (Vallespin, 2000, pp. 156 ss.). Un Estado catalizador de la sociedad, impulsor del desarrollo social, político y económico, si bien regido por la política interna y externa y no sólo por la economía. Un Estado preocupado por construir una «sociedad decente», en la que las instituciones no humillen a las personas, y una «sociedad civilizada», en la que sus miembros no se humillan unos a otros."

Corruption is not a new phenomenon. It is the age of mankind on Earth.

The attitude that seems most coherent to those who investigate this issue is not to ignore the existence of corruption nor to propose its extinction, but rather to seek means that will help to enable man to face the temptation to subjugate his neighbor, mainly when this comes from those who are to serve the public treasury and not to plunder it. Those who love their country do not loot it because historically looting comes from an enemy.

If, in fact, we consider that ethics, morality, and law create men who are more resistant to greed, we must fight against corruption with all the force that the State has, for, as Nietzsche said (2007: 141) *"Los enfermos son el máximo peligro para los sanos; no de los más fuertes les viene la desgracia a los fuertes, sino de los más débiles."*

If we are not prepared to fight for the maximum reduction of State corruption, we will have to assume the full contradiction between what the State says it is and what it really is. On the other hand, if the modern State is unable to reduce corruption to tolerable levels, then it needs to give way to an institution that will be able to do it.

CHAPTER 3

Causes of Corruption

Causalism and finalism fascinate and keep men alive in their quest for happiness, whether from the point of view of Aristotelian Eudemonia, Hedonistic Epicureanism, or utilitarianism as defended by Jeremy Bentham.

In the process of rationalizing individual or collective happiness, the perception of corruption is only a movement of the soul that cannot be confused with social well-being.

Social welfare is a rationalized perception from life in society proposed, above all, by the liberal State. In this context, corruption appears as an obstacle because it emerges as an opposing force not only to the promise, but also to the capacity for achieving freedom, equality, and social fraternity. That is why we need to question daily the role and speech of the ones who hold the power.

Why does man corrupt and allow himself to be corrupted? Where are the roots of the phenomenon? Is corruption in man as an "original sin" as creationism wants? Does it come from the fight between the strongest and the weakest, as evolutionism accentuates? Does it reside in the State, as anarchism wants? After all, what are the causes of corruption?

Marilena Chaui (1988; 11-13) when analyzing the relation of cause and effect says:

> "Modern thinking reduced the four causes to only two: the efficient and the final, giving to the word 'cause' the sense we give it today, that is, an operation or an action. Modern physics considers that Nature acts in a completely

mechanical way, as a necessary system of cause and effect relations, taking the cause always and exclusively in the sense of motive or efficient cause. Therefore, there are no final causes in Nature. On the field of metaphysics, however, besides the efficient cause, the final cause is preserved since it refers to all voluntary and free action, i.e., it refers to the action of God and that of men. The will (divine and human) is free and acts in view of goals or objectives to be achieved."

Héctor A. Mairal(2007: 91-93) studying *"Las raíces legales de la corrupción"* emphasizes that *"Es necesario destruir las causas que la favorecen."* He speaks almost like a doctor who knows that healing the pain does not solve the patient's problem. It is necessary to find the cause and exterminate it. He further adds:

"Obviamente, la corrupción no anida solamente en el Estado: *It takes two to tango.* Solo en los albores de la historia se castigaba únicamente al funcionario corrupto y no al particular que lo sobornaba. El Estado presenta similares características a las de la sociedad que lo constituye. Por ello, no es solo el aparato estatal al que hay que controlar.

Pero también, en un proceso de continua interacción, la sociedad misma se va modelando de acuerdo con los estímulos que recibe del Estado. Un Estado corrupto es, en cierta medida, producto de la corrupción que existe en el seno de la sociedad, pero a su vez en esta el grado de corrupción aumenta en la medida que se advierte no solo que ella ayuda a ganar posiciones frente al Estado y frente a la competencia, sino que es ella misma considerada conducta valiosa: 'La internalización de una mentalidad transgresora es vivida en muchas ocasiones como un signo vernáculo de vivacidad e, incluso, de brillo personal, sin advertirse que tal comportamiento degrada individualmente a quien lo practica y, a la vez, se proyecta socialmente como un desvalor comunitario, el cual, en una retroalimentación perversa, gravita sobre la conciencia individual neutralizándola o deformándola.' Nada es más descorazonador para una persona, un funcionario, un investigador, un empresario, honestos, que descubrir que otros han triunfado gracias a maniobras incorrectas e ilegales. El mensaje que el Estado envía así a la población es deletéreo: Ahuyenta a los mejores y premia a los peores. (...)

El mejoramiento del comportamiento ético del Estado tendría efectos directos en la población, creando un círculo virtuoso en el cual los estímulos y premios están orientados a promover la excelencia y no la deshonestidad. Sin embargo, para alcanzarlo no bastan las exhortaciones éticas dirigidas a los funcionarios. Se atribuye a Stalin la frase que con una docena de San Francisco de Asís no hubiera acaecido la revolución rusa. Las soluciones que requieren un cambio de la naturaleza humana son propias de las religiones y no de las ciencias sociales. Es de la naturaleza humana reaccionar de manera bastante similar al tipo de estímulos que recibe. Cambiemos el sistema, que la gran mayoría de las personas se ajustaran al nuevo sistema, no por haber ellos mismos cambiado, sino porque se adecuaran a los nuevos estímulos.

Concluimos, por ello, que no es suficiente con combatir los efectos de la corrupción. Es necesario destruir las causas que la favorecen, entre las cuales las más fácilmente corregibles son las legales. La corrección de los factores jurídicos que alientan la corrupción y que venimos de listar no la eliminaría totalmente, pero reduciría su campo de acción en los casos en los que actualmente se recurre a ella ante la falta de mecanismos correcto de solución de conflictos frente al Estado, o en los que el derecho crea innecesariamente la oportunidad para que exista. Decimos innecesariamente porque siempre habrá favores oficiales cuya concesión, o normas restrictivas cuya no aplicación, otorgara beneficios a quien obtiene irregularmente ese favor o dispensa. Lo que se trata es determinar en qué casos el favor o la restricción legal deberían eliminarse por desvaliosos, ya sea porque no acarrean ventajas significativas para la sociedad (aunque las acarre en para el funcionario) o, cuando menos, porque sus consecuencias sociales negativas superan las positivas. Al así hacerlo estaremos simultáneamente reduciendo las oportunidades para que florezca la corrupción."

It is a fact that corruption is not only based in the State and that it takes two to tango. In the symbiosis between the public and the private, it is undeniable that society is modeling itself by the stimuli that it receives and that the improvement of the ethical behavior of the State will have direct ethical effects on the population.

Mairal assumes that if the State is corrupt, man will also be corrupt, and, for that, the first must be controlled. It is a closer idea of Friedrich Engels's thinking when he says that the State exposes our incapacities and weaknesses.

In describing corruption in Argentina, Mairal (2007: 15-20) states:

"En la Argentina se tiene la percepción, apoyada en datos de la realidad y confirmada por encuestas nacionales e internacionales, que su difusión es muy alta, incluso en comparación con países vecinos y de similares características sociales, económicas y culturales: 'El fenómeno de la corrupción esta masivamente generalizado en la sociedad argentina' afirmaba CARLOS NINO en 1992, mientras que Luis MORENO OCAMPO ha calificado a la situación argentina de hipercorrupcion. De acuerdo con una encuesta Gallup de 1996, el 97% del público del Gran Buenos Aires consideraba que el nivel de corrupción en Argentina es alto o muy alto, mientras que Transparency International colocaba a Argentina en el puesto 35 entre 54 países ordenados de menor a mayor según su nivel de corrupción, significativamente detrás de Chile (N° 21), resultado que se repetía en un índice preparado por la misma organización y en el cual con un índice de 3 para el año 1998 (de un máximo de 10 para los países en los que no se observan prácticas corruptas como ocurre con Nueva Zelanda), Argentina estaba detrás de Chile (6,8), Uruguay (4,3) y aun de Brasil (4). La percepción desde entonces no ha mejorado. (...)

En su clásica obra El Otro Sendero, HERNADO DE SOTO es elocuente en la crítica a lo que denomina derecho redistributivo que surge cuando el derecho es concebido 'como un instrumento para redistribuir la riqueza y no para facilitar su creación.' No debería sorprender, dice este autor, 'que el soborno y la corrupción sean características resultantes de un sistema de derecho en el cual la competencia por las rentas se ha convertido en la forma predominante de producir la ley.' Estas palabras parecen ser escritas para nuestro país, que durante el año 2002 vivió una avalancha normativa que, cual la lotería de Babilonia que imaginó BORGES, empobreció a diversos sectores de la población y enriqueció a otros.

Más recientemente, en una visión crítica de ciertos aspectos del proceso de privatización en Latinoamérica, se ha advertido que la corrupción puede también encontrar oportunidades y desarrollarse tanto durante la etapa de privatización misma como en la subsiguiente etapa regulatoria. Hay quienes dan por sentado que la corrupción crece en los gobiernos de derecha. ( )

El presente trabajo constituye, por ello, un intento de describir algunos de los factores jurídicos que operan como caldo de cultivo o, incluso, como causa directa de la corrupción, independientemente del sistema económico o político imperante, y apuntar preliminarmente algunos posibles remedios. Observamos, desde ya, que el problema excede a un determinado régimen o partido. Situaciones como las que describimos en el presente vienen Teniendo lugar en nuestro país desde hace décadas. ( )

El enfoque propuesto es distinto del generalmente seguido cuando se intenta combatir la corrupción por medios jurídicos, aunque complementario con él. Estos medios, par lo común., bus can desalentar la corrupción a través de la sanción a las culpables, para lo cual establecen obligaciones de diverso tipo para las funcionarios públicos, tipifican delitos, establecen penas, imponen incompatibilidades, prohibiciones y controles, permiten presunciones y adoptan otras medidas de disuasión y persecución. Así ocurre con las leyes que se han dictado en nuestro país en estos últimos años y con los tratados que durante esos mismos años ha aprobado el Congreso. Por el contrario, no se suele prestar atención al marco jurídico que fomenta la corrupción ni a los posibles remedios para evitar tal consecuencia y, en lo posible, prevenirla. Sin embargo, el enfoque que se propone no carece de utilidad: 'Para evitar la corrupción - dice Luis MORENO OCAMPO - es más importante detectar sistemas culpables que personas culpables."

The ranking of the most corrupt countries in the world does not change much. In Latin America, it almost always changes for the worse, with the exception of Uruguay that has been maintaining lower levels for the region.

Luis Moreno Ocampo says that in order to avoid corruption it is more important to identify guilty systems than guilty people. One does not see how to separate people from systems. Everything works in a symbiosis in which one does not exist without the other. So blaming the system sounds more like an excuse than a solution.

The social system, whichever it may be, is galvanized by conduct, which, in turn, translates into human action or omission directed to a particular end.

To live in society is to live in association with micro-social systems. Such practice sometimes leads men to associate with one another in order to protect their personal interests and those for whom they are interested.

Manuel Villoria Mendieta (2000: 100) maintains that a correct social analysis of corruption must begin with the practices that a certain society regards as corrupt or not. This is how this idea is supported:

> "Un análisis científico de la corrupción tiene que partir de lo que la sociedad en cuestión considera como corrupto y, a partir de ahí, estudiar (Leys, 1989):
>
> 1) El nivel de asunción de los propósitos oficiales por parte de las instituciones sociales y sus miembros, así como la fortaleza de asunciones rivales, por ejemplo, la asunción de que es preciso

ayudar a los familiares frente a la igualdad y merito en el acceso a la Función Pública.

2) La extensión hasta la que la acción que contraviene los criterios oficiales es vista como corrupta.

3) Los incentivos y desincentivos que para corrompe r a un empleado público existen.

4) La facilidad con la que la corrupción - una vez definida es llevada a cabo."

Víctor Manuel Monti (1999: 79-80), in turn, joins sociological and economic factors as causes of corruption. In addressing poverty, cultural heritage, and failures in the education of society states:

"Entre las diversas cosas que se dicen acerca de la raíz del problema, es que la corrupción es producto de la pobreza; empero, la pobreza puede jugar un rol, pero difícilmente pueda ser la causa principal. Se invoca esta excusa incluso, para justificar el otorgamiento de sustanciosas remuneraciones y compensaciones a magistrados y funcionarios porque de esta manera - se sostiene - no se verían necesitados ni tentados a obtener recursos par medios ilícitos. Empero, la experiencia indica que suele ocurrir que las prácticas fraudulentas y corruptas encuentran campo tertil justamente en aquellos que ocupan los más altos escalones de la jerarquía económica de la sociedad, y, desde luego, de la burocracia del estado. Contrastan estos individuos y funcionario con otros peor pagos que han mantenido siempre su integridad e incorruptibilidad.

Otro argumento reiteradamente expuesto encuadrando ya la cuestión en el ámbito latinoamericano, es que la corrupción en nuestros países es el producto de una herencia cultural cuyos valores éticos y morales - que serían bastante laxos - harían de los latinos sujetos tolerante s de la corrupción. Este argumento es una extensión de la tesis que nuestro subdesarrollo obedece a razones culturales ancestrales. Sus promotores pretenden confirmar esta tesis señalando que a diferencia nuestra, los países del norte de América recibieron una «herencia cultural» distinta, fueron colonizados par la cultura anglosajona que trajo consigo valores morales y conceptos éticos que les permitieron crear sociedades desarrolladas.

Otros, simplifican diciendo que corrupción es el producto de una constante debilidad y deshonestidad humana, debido a la carencia de patrones morales y éticos. Incluso, la sociología y la antropología han pretendido encontrar explicaciones a la corrupción n en razones de índole cultural.

Sin pretender dejar de lado que la cultura y la educación están íntimamente vinculados a las causas de la corrupción, creemos que los diagnósticos expuestos no constituyen una respuesta integral y suficiente para resolver el problema. También se sostiene y no sin razón, que también contribuye con la corrupción la existencia de organizaciones (dependencia publica, empresa, institución social) cuyo funciona miento, así ramo la interrelación entre las individuos que la integran y los usuarios se encuentran reguladas por un conjunto de normas que según coma se encuentren concebidas pueden favorecer, promover o desalentar los actos marginales a las formalidades consagradas por esas normas."

Fortunately, Monti (1999: 82, 84) does not yield to dogmatism. He admits that poverty, cultural heritage, and flaws in education are some, but not the only causes of corruption.

The author shares the truths of other scholars of the field who have identified corruption as an endemic disease and, thus, advance in his considerations, as true for Argentina as for Brazil and for any country in the world. His point of view:

"Moreno Ocampo cita a la obra de Robin Theobald, Corrupción, desarrollo y subdesarrollo», quien se ocupa de demostrar que «la hipercorrupcion es un fenómeno que agobia a los países más pobres o desorganizados. Estos países exhiben situaciones de abuso de poder y de corrupción cualitativa y cuantitativamente superiores a las de los países desarrollados. La nota característica es un Estado que funciona con muy bajo nivel de calidad.» (Moreno Ocampo, 1993, pág. 120) (...)

Grondona describe este panorama de la siguiente manera: «E n los países subdesarrollados (...) la corrupción es intensa tanto en los estratos altos como en los medios y bajos: infecta al Estado en su totalidad. Comienza con el policía que pide una coima para no multar una infracción en el transito, sigue con los funcionarios de la Aduana que cobran para ignorar las leves impositivas y asciende hasta contaminar las conductas de los altos funcionarios. Diríamos entonces, según la terminología que hemos adoptado, que mientras en los países desarrollados hay actos de corrupción, sobre todo en las altas esferas del poder, los países subdesarrollados padecen un estado de corrupción. (...)

Según Juan Bautista y Juan de Dios Cincunegui, haciendo la salvedad que «...cada país posee peculiaridades propias, pueden detallarse tres factores generales determinantes de la corrupción: el dinero; la situación de pobreza; y la política.» Según estos autores, se advierte que la acumulación de riqueza hoy en día no es un producto proporcional del trabajo; que el manejo desaprensivo de los fondos públicos puestos estos al servicio de la actividad política constituye una grave corrupción; se compromete el desarrollo de la nación con el desgaste grosero de los fondos del estado. (Cincunegui, 1996, pág. 143/4)."

3.1 – Money, Poverty, Politics

Monti joins Juan Bautista and Juan de Dios Cincunegui when defending that each country has its own peculiarities, but three factors are determinants of corruption: money, poverty, and politics.

Daniel Kahneman, Nobel Prize in Economic Sciences in 2002, says in a speech available on YouTube that money does not buy happiness, but the lack of it produces poverty.

Money has the power to buy almost everything. It even had the power to buy men in the slavery market.

Poverty, in turn, makes man capable of selling his own soul to reach the money that favors a minimum of well-being which, as a rule, he confuses with happiness.

Politics, in turn, is merciless. It is the most powerful intellectual tool that man has ever built and perfected. Behold, he took charge of the word, by which creationism says that the worlds were made, and created a god called the State and with it a whole political theology to indoctrinate and dogmatize its dominion.

Political-state dogmas have created the sign of "popular representation" whose meaning is to let third parties who do not know us and do not know about our existence or who distance themselves as soon as elected, speak for us, travel for us, drink for us, eat for us, and live a full life for us, though most of this imaginary collective live in misery and blame its ancestors for it.

Perhaps this is one of the strongest reasons why the failure of public policies is always transferred to third parties. The political utilitarianism uses the Eve complex or transference of guilt syndrome and blames our ancestors for corruption calling it cultural heritage. This thesis of corruption as a cultural heritage would not be valid if further investigated.

The already cited The Almanac of Political Corruption, Scandals & Dirty Politics shows how the corruption of the North Americans came nested in the English settlers. Below is another enlightening excerpt from the Almanac (2007: 1):

> "Is this perception appropriate, much less accurate? One of the goals of this project is to provide a new measuring rod with which to gauge the breadth and depth of the current political environment, both the activities of politicians and the process of electing them. A chronological history—from our colonial roots onward—provides just such a unique barometer of reality. And it becomes quickly apparent, once this approach is underway, that the past provides a considerable wealth of evidence to support the folk saying, "The more things change, the more they stay the same."

Pick any category of modern political wrongdoing—
sins of the flesh, theft, bribery, extortion, lies, cover-ups,
election fraud—and historical precedents are easy to find.
Add an element missing from most political activity in
the past few decades, bloodshed, and the historical record
often outshines today's antics.

Yet our human inclination to focus on the sensational
does us a disservice. Even in colonial America, people
read newspapers, the main source of information about
current events, but then, as now, "normal" isn't news. As
the saying goes, it's only news when the man bites the dog.
The current and historical record of political misdoings
covers just that, misdoings, not the standard, mundane,
day-to-day operations that keep local and national systems
operational."

In summary, it is worth to highlight the last but one paragraph that
states:

"Choose any category of modern political offense,
such as sins of the flesh, bribery, robbery, extortion,
lies, cover-ups, election fraud, and it will be easy to find
historical precedents..."

In the investigation of causes and factors of corruption, we must credit
David Baigun and Nicolás García Rivas (2006: 121-123) for the following
citation:

"Desde la realidad colombiana, señala Avila Bernal,
con relación a la corrupción pública, es posible señalar tres
aspectos esenciales:

a) La corrupción es tanto más intensa y generalizada
cuanto que se genera en el seno de una sociedad parasita
con una economía improductiva, diferenciando la
corrupción desde el exterior y la autóctona.
b) La corrupción es el fiel reflejo del carácter irracional
de la planificación y se traduce, finalmente, por

la aplicación desordenada y parcial del plan o del documento considerado como tal.

c) La corrupción no es sino la manifestación concreta de un Estado frágil, el cual, para protegerse y mantenerse necesita desarrollar nuevas formas de corrupción y consolidar el cinismo como instrumento de poder. (RIVAS, Nicolas Garcia (dir.). Delincuencia económica y corrupción. 1. ed. Buenos Aires: Ediar.)"

Guillermo Ariel Todarello (2008: 131-133,139) also contributes to the study of the causes of corruption by highlighting factors such as:

"I. Factor educacional

(...) es imprescindible tener en consideración que, en términos generales, la mayor parte de las conductas desviadas o antisociales encuentran su germen en la deficiente educación recibida por aquellos autores que deciden desplegar voluntariamente dicho acto prohibido. (...)

II. Aspectos culturales que favorecen la corrupción

En realidad, la mayor parte de los países en desarrollo se encuentran conformados por sociedades donde las lealtades grupales o de parentesco constituyen un motivo trascendente capaz de relegar o apartar las obligaciones de un agente con respecto a sus deberes públicos, creando de esta manera un clima propicio para el desarrollo de la corrupción administrativa. ( )

III. Normas culturales en la Argentina

Por otro lado, se considera que el despliegue de un manejo eficiente de elementos tales como el ardid y la astucia en el marco de las diferentes relaciones sociales, constituye un valor central en la cultura argentina, la cual si bien no premia la corrupción en forma explícita, desplaza los límites morales, considerando al menos aceptable un comportamiento que en otro contexto valorativo seria censurable. La valoración y encumbramiento de elementos relacionados con la sagacidad y el oportunismo por sobre el esfuerzo y la honestidad, junto a una exaltación de la cultura de la renta, configuran un ambiente propicio para la generación de aquellas conductas destinadas a la búsqueda de beneficios materiales urgentes."

Todarello asserts that in Argentina deficiencies in education, embellishment, sagacity, and opportunism, when placed above personal effort and honesty, together with a culture of profit, constitute the perfect environment to the generalization of acts aimed at seeking material benefits.

In this pursuit, personal interests end up prevailing over collective interests. There is no doubt this reality plagues the peripheral and developing countries of the American continent.

Héctor A. Mairal (2007: 50-52, 55-57, 59-62) lists causes of corruption worth mentioning:

"3.1. Las normas irreales o excesivamente ambiciosas

La existencia de normas cuyo cumplimiento es prácticamente imposible, muy dificultoso o muy costoso ha sido identificada por HERNANDO DE SOTO como una importante causa de corrupción dado que el soborno constituye el costo que paga el empresario informal para evitar la sanción y poder así permanecer en la actividad. El fenómeno ha sido estudiado también en Brasil. En nuestro país, decía NINO, al analizar las causas de la corrupción, 'Hay normas que exigen obligaciones de cumplimiento casi imposible o absurdo' y daba como ejemplo las normas para habilitación de negocios que imponen recaudos exagerados. Semilleros de corrupción ha llamado VANOSSI a los excesos reglamentarios.

Lo mismo ocurre con las normas demasiado ambiciosas que trasladan sobre algunos particulares el costo del mejoramiento social al que ellas - comprensible pero a veces algo desaprensivamente - aspiran. Tal lo que sucede con las normas de urbanismo, sindicadas por NETO como una frecuente fuente de corrupción: Como el valor de un terreno varia dramáticamente según la decisión discrecional del funcionario u órgano colegiado que aplica las normas sobre zonificación, es optimista esperar que la corrupción este ausente en la adopción de esa decisión. Algo similar se ha observado con las normas de saneamiento ambiental impuestas en sistemas en los que la corrupción es generalizada: 'Usualmente es más barato sobornar al funcionario que realizar las mejoras.'(...)

Por ello, un país como la Argentina, cuya sociedad demuestra un alto grado de corrupción y una fuerte renuencia al cumplimiento de la ley, debiera tener ambiciones modestas al fijar los objetivos de sus normas cuando los valores en juego no sean la vida o la salud de las personas. Imponer nuevas y ambiciosas regulaciones sin prever el aumento del gasto publico necesario para controlar su cumplimiento, equivale a estimular la corrupción. Por ello, cuando se establezcan metas ambiciosas deberán preverse sistemas de control eficientes y permanentes con su correspondiente asignación presupuestaria. De lo contrario se castigara a los buenos ciudadanos, obligándolos al cumplimiento de onerosos deberes, y se premiara a los malos ciudadanos, tolerando su incumplimiento por pasividad o colusión. ( )

El exceso reglamentario (*regulatory overshoot*) deriva en nuestro país, en gran medida, de la concepción de la ley como un objetivo de mejoramiento social y no como un mínimo de conducta efectivamente exigible. 'La concepción subyacente a esta actitud es la de la ley como un ideal colectivo puro, maravilloso, pero en definitiva remoto e inaplicable.' Como dice ERNESTO GARZON VALDES: 'Los latinoamericanos solemos ser expertos en el cultivo de la dimensión simbólica de las leyes.' En lugar de establecer pautas realistas que recién con el correr del tiempo pueden irse haciendo más exigentes, se establecen ab initio requerimientos cumplibles solo por unos pocos. Las normas se dictan sabiendo que no podrán ser respetadas pero esperando que su mera existencia vaya llevando a sus destinatarios, gradualmente, a adecuar su conducta a las nuevas exigencias. Frecuentemente ellas se copian de leyes de países extranjeros más adelantados, sin analizar previamente su real compatibilidad con las condiciones en que se desenvuelve la sociedad argentina. Pero ocurre que la versión argentina es, a veces, aun más rigurosa que el original, demostrando así que el efecto que se persigue al sancionar la norma es demostrar el celo de legisladores o funcionarios más que establecer pautas razonables de conducta. Colocar en estado de incumplimiento general a los particulares no es problema que parezca quitar el sueño a los autores de las normas argentinas. (...)

3.2. El exceso en el otorgamiento de facultades discrecionales

La corrupción tiene por objeto, comúnmente, aprovechar el ejercicio de las facultades discrecionales de la administración pública en interés privado, sea de un particular o del funcionario interviniente, o de ambos. Por ello, cuanto mayor sea la discrecionalidad, mayor serán las oportunidades para que la corrupción aparezca: '[L]a discrecionalidad es el mejor caldo de cultivo de corrupciones.' Monopolio mas discrecionalidad menos transparencia es la clásica formula de KLITGAARD para medir el grado de corrupción en un sistema.

Obviamente, un determinado grado de discrecionalidad es no solo inevitable sino también deseable, toda vez que la norma no puede fijar rígidamente la conducta que el Estado debe seguir ante cada situación y el rol del administrador publico exige normalmente la elección de alternativas. En el accionar de la administración pública, la existencia de facultades discrecionales es un fenómeno necesario a tal punto que la doctrina ha dedicado innumerables páginas a su limitación, pero nunca a su erradicación. Como dice DAVIS '[n]o podemos alcanzar los principales objetivos del gobierno moderno sin facultades discrecionales significativas.' ( )

3.2.1. La discrecionalidad en la selección de los controlados

La arbitrariedad en la selección de los particulares a ser objeto de control administrativo y, en su caso, de sanción, es un fenómeno que, desgraciadamente, ocurre más a menudo de lo que se cree. La selección de 'vedettes penales' es una práctica advertida por algunos autores, mientras que otros destacan, como factor de corrupción, 'la opción sobre los sectores a inspeccionar." En nuestro país frecuentemente se investiga a particulares cuyo grado de cumplimiento es claramente superior a la media del sector, lo que demuestra parcialidad en la determinación del universo que será objeto de control y abre la puerta al uso de los mecanismos estatales de control con fines de presión o persecución política. Así, una cadena de supermercados, uno de los principales contribuyentes del país, cuyos locales de venta y depósito son modelo de higiene, es objeto de continuas inspecciones sanitarias y de otro tipo que buscan aplicarle sanciones de clausura, las que sistemáticamente son dejadas sin efecto por la justicia. En los Estados Unidos (porque esta práctica viciosa ciertamente no se limita a nuestro país) se ha considerado violatorio de la Primera Enmienda, que el gobierno inicie acciones retaliatorias, incluso procesamientos penales, contra quienes lo critican. (...)

Si bien la exageración en la presión fiscal o en otras medidas oficiales favorece la corrupción, las empresas pueden de todos modos desenvolverse bajo tales medidas cuando el control de los incumplimientos es eficaz y general. Lo que mantenimiento de niveles éticos en la actividad privada es la política de discriminación en los controles o, lo que en definitiva conduce a similares resultados, la imposición de cargas y restricciones cuyo cumplimiento el Estado sabe que será solo parcial y podrá controlar en pocos casos. No es solo el rigor de la norma lo que afecta el nivel de corrupción sino, fundamentalmente, la conciencia de que será aplicada discrecionalmente.

3.2.2. La multiplicidad de habilitaciones especiales

En una reunión en Chile en que se analizaban posibles medidas regulatorias, un consultor argentino propuso que, como medida de control, se exigieran autorizaciones administrativas especiales para realizar ciertas actividades menores. La reacción de los funcionarios de ese país fue unánime: 'En Chile hemos aprendido que las autorizaciones especiales generan corrupción. Por ello lo correcto es establecer en forma general las condiciones que deben reunirse para llevar a cabo ciertas actividades y controlar luego si quienes las desempeñan cumplen o no con esas condiciones.'

En Argentina no parecen existir escrúpulos similares, a juzgar por las numerosas normas que exigen autorizaciones especiales. Por ello, uno de los métodos para reducir el nivel de corrupción es eliminar - donde sea posible - las exigencias de habilitaciones, permisos y demás autorizaciones administrativas, reemplazándolas por otras medidas de control. (...)

También desde este punto de vista es preferible la competencia (allí donde es posible) a la regulación, ya que evita la necesidad de decisiones administrativas discrecionales que pueden ser distorsionadas por la corrupción. Similarmente, si se debe controlar la entrada a una industria (por vía de licencias, autorizaciones o medidas análogas), será más transparente un sistema que disponga el otorgamiento de licencia a todo quien se encuentre en las condiciones fijadas por ley o reglamento basado en ley, que otro que permita a la autoridad otorgarlas o denegarlas, según su apreciación discrecional del mercado o del requirente. ( )

3.2.3. La demora en resolver

La respuesta que da el derecho argentino a estas situaciones es pobre y la burocracia la ha empobrecido aun más. La regla general es que el silencio ante la petición del particular implica negativa, a menos que una norma establezca que el silencio implica consentimiento. Esto último ocurre en algunos pocos casos, tal como la citada aprobación de la autoridad de aplicación de la Ley de Defensa de la Competencia que se considera otorgada si no recae una negativa expresa dentro de los 45 días de efectuada la presentación. Sin embargo, este plazo resulta inoperante en la práctica ante la facultad del organismo de suspenderlo solicitando mayor información.

Aquí cabria una primera observación. La regla general del silencio administrativo interpretado coma negativa es correcta cuando se la aplica a presentaciones espontaneas de las particulares, pues de lo contrario el Estado se vería inundado de peticiones infundadas en la esperanza de que quedaran consentidas par el mero silencio. Pero no lo es cuando el pedido de aprobación lo exige la misma ley: En este caso, el silencio debería considerarse aprobación, luego de un plazo razonable. Si el Estado somete a las particulares a la molestia, demora y costo de someter su transacción al vista bueno oficial, debiera poner a disposición las medias para que el trámite sea razonablemente rápido. Y si el Estado omite crear el organismo de control, la solución no es paralizar la actividad privada hasta que ello ocurra (como parecerían pretender algunos fallos), sino no aplicar la ley restrictiva."

3.2 — Unreal Laws, Infeasible Laws, and Excess of Regulation

For Héctor Mairal, these are causes of corruption:

1 - unreal laws;

2 - infeasible laws;

3 - the excessive regulation or discretionary faculties promoted by the State;

4 - a deliberate delay in the decision-making process. Holding back processes so that the decision seems difficult and the petitioner has to bribe someone to see a request being met. It is a formula invented by the public officer to be seen as mediator between the supposed problem and the solution and, thus, be considered worthy of the "reward."

Professor António Manuel Hespanha (2005: 86) in his book *"Cultura jurídica européia"* says that what man produces must be linked to his inner self. Here is what he says:

> "On the contrary, we insist that the practices that history deals with are practices of men, somehow resulting from acts of cognition, affectivity, evaluation, and volition. At any of these levels of mental activity presupposed by action are clear moments of choice, in which agents construct versions of the external world, evaluate them, choose between alternative forms of reaction, represent the results, and anticipate future consequences. All these operations belong to the sphere of the inner world. They are irreducibly intellectual operations based on representations constructed by the agent eventually from stimuli (of varied nature) received from the outside."

We do not intend to make this work an eristic dialectic (the art of arguing and always being right). Our real desire is to achieve logic in reasoning because it pursues the content or essence of the studied object.

In investigating the causes of corruption, our desire is to prove its existence by identifying its source and, thus, to create a path for the most fertile minds to propose solutions. If we help ourselves, justice may prevail.

Because we agree with Professor Manuel Hespanha, without, however, not denying the other transcribed truths, we think that the best course in this logical journey on the causes of corruption is to believe that the internal factor (the will) is the most decisive of all inducers of corruption. It is in each individual's conscience that free will is associated with the criminal action and omission directed to a certain end.

This is why the finalist theory of action in criminal law, for example, considers every action or omission as a crime, without making any judgment on the guile or guilt that motivates conduct.

Conduct *per se* is enough, that is, action or omission directed to a specific criminal purpose, so that the State has the right to install *jus persecuendi* and *jus puniendi* against the offender.

Brazilian and Latin American administrative laws consider cases of deviations from functional conduct. In the specific case of Brazil, it absorbs from the criminal process almost the fullness of its rite, adopting, even, the principle of real truth in the instruction of the administrative disciplinary process.

Those who err for absolute ignorance are excusable because they do not know how to act. Whoever errs under the realm of the knowledge of the truth must bear the consequences.

In a State governed by the rule of law, the consequences may be criminal, administrative, and civil penalties provided for by law considering the law has not been manipulated from the outset in favor of the system of institutionalized corruption under the disguise of party politics.

CHAPTER 4

Consequences of Corruption

The topic is complex since there are factors that can be considered simultaneously the cause and the consequence of corruption, such as hunger and fear.

A hungry person is vulnerable to bribery (hunger as a cause), and whoever sacks the public resources causes hunger to whom public policy should feed (hunger as a consequence).

Fear as a synonym of insecurity for an economic future can lead someone to become corrupt (fear as a cause), just as the fear felt by a new employee in a public office full of corrupts can lead this new employee to also become corrupt (fear as a consequence).

On the other hand, hunger and fear of the future are undeniable consequences in the lives of those who are relegated by the State to a state of misery. Giovanni Berlinger and Volnei Garrafa (1996: 119) support this truth with the following words:

> "The second aspect concerns present and future relations between rich and poor countries. A great Brazilian scientist and politician, Josué de Castro, who, as president of the FAO (Food and Agriculture Organization of the United Nations), and as a writer, was, in the 50s, the first to disclose to the world the geography and geopolitics of hunger. He meant that humanity is divided into two groups: that of those who do not eat, and those who do not sleep because their conscience is heavy, mainly because of fear that the hungry may rebel."

Eradicating misery by relegating poverty and corruption to acceptable levels should be one of the main goals of the State. In the Mercosur area, for example, Brazil is cited as an example of economic success by the middle of this century, according to the CIA Report (2006: 139). Here is an excerpt from the work:

> "Experts acknowledge that Brazil is a pivotal state with a vibrant democracy, a diversified economy and entrepreneurial population, a large national patrimony, and solid economic institutions. Brazil's success or failure in balancing pro-growth economic measures with an ambitious social agenda that reduces poverty and income inequality will have a profound impact on region-wide economic performance and governance during the next 14 years."

However, economic success without political will is like the weapon without the ammunition. Julio E.S. Virgolini (2004: 258) says that *"El problema de la corrupción es esencialmente político, y su consecuencia más relevante es que desemboca en un proceso de exclusión."*

As a matter of fact and a matter of law, if we wish to be developed nations within Mercosur and other communities of nations, we must replace the culture of corruption with a civic feeling of respect for human rights.

It should be understood that I am not making reference to the "human rights of lawbreakers", as many associations claim, believing that crime stems only from poverty or deficiency in education.

Most people in the world are poor and yet have not elected to kill, steal, or destroy, despite their not desired socioeconomic status or poor educational process. To use social circumstances as causes for marginality is naivety.

History is full with refutations to the thesis of these groups for whom the lawbreakers deserve all respect and society must take all the blame for their criminal actions.

Anyone who thinks this way is naive or ill-intentioned because conduct is any conscious action or omission directed towards a particular purpose, and whoever consciously and consciously conducts himself to crime must respond to his or her culpability.

When I am referring to human rights, I wish to reinforce the call for the fulfillment of the promises of social welfare made by the modern state, of which I cite Article 6 of the Constitution of the Federative Republic of Brazil, which says that *"social rights are education, health, food, work, housing, leisure, security, social security, maternity and child protection, assistance to the needy..."*

For Virgolini, if someone benefits from corruption, someone else loses. The ones who lose are the lower and middle classes that are the recipients of public benefits since the upper class is in the power.

We need to motivate the culture that ethics produces better consequences than corruption, albeit in the long run, reaffirming daily to society that corruption destroys the moral and economic foundations of a nation and that its ransom consumes decades of education.

Corruption inevitably produces poverty and misery as a consequence. It is a matter of cause and effect. A result follows one or several causes, given the relationship of dependence invoked by the *conditio sine qua non* theory, as inferred, for example, from the Brazilian Criminal Code:

> "Article 13 - The result, on which the existence of the
> crime depends, is attributable only to the one who caused
> it. It is considered cause the action or omission without
> which the result would not have occurred."

Corruption has become so subtle among Mercosur member countries that the phrase "one steals, but does a little" has subverted the ethical order that should exist between the honesty of the agent in the performance of the duties of the office, employment, or term, and the practice of act of corruption in the exercise thereof.

In other words, corruption has become such a strong system that common sense accepts that if the public agent performs some of his campaign promises or what the law foresees as his duties, he may corrupt and be corrupted and it shall be justified. The question is: who benefits from this message?

Note that the phrase "one steals, but does a little", so commonplace in Brazil, for example, is permeated by two findings. The first is that the public agent is a corrupt and the second that he does, that is, he fulfills the duties of the position, job, or term. From any point of view, the two conducts are distinct and there can be no acceptable connection between them, at least ethically.

For ethics what is evil cannot be good and vice versa. Just as for law what is typified as a crime is forbidden. For example, if a public official receives a bribe to approve a project to build public housing, the end is good because the poor need housing, but bribery as a means is not justified in the supposed humanity or pity of the bribed.

Likewise, a public agent receives bribes to release an irregular environmental permit for the construction of a hydroelectric power plant to supply the country's industrial sector deficiency. Does the completion of the project mean that the public agent acted ethically? Could the corrupt conduct that hastened the construction of the power plant with speed and perfection be considered ethical, moral, or legal?

The positive result achieved is infected by the virus of corruption. It looks good from the outside perspective, but it is rotten in its principles. At least, this is the message of the democratic states that consider themselves guardians of the principle of legality.

Still, in relation to the above examples, it could be said that being efficiency the art of quick, productive, and adequate administration, bribery would have been a means to that end. However, could such an end have been achieved without the bribe simply for the duty of fidelity to the position to which the public agent is responsible? The answer is undoubtedly YES!

Usually, those who corrupt disapprove of the conduct of those who allow themselves to be corrupted, but are always happy with the result achieved because one is the condemnation of the act of corruption, and the other is the happiness for the gift reached with the act of corruption. This happens because in a nationalist socialist utilitarian logic, the means justify the ends.

In this collection, we defend the notion that corruption is a deviance of reprehensible conduct, without making any concessions because we understand that public agents that corrupt themselves with little do so because they have little power, yet not little greed.

David Baigun (2006: 121-123) lists twenty-two political and legal consequences of corruption, as follows:

"Méndez relaciona el subdesarrollo con la corrupción, indicando cuales son algunas de las consecuencias institucionales de la misma. Así, señala:

a. Los sectores políticos y económicos más poderosos se excluyen del sistema legal en cuanto este amenace o perjudique sus intereses.

b. La cohesión social se pierde. La población se divide entre los sectores minoritarios que rodean a las familias gobernantes y/o hombres fuertes de turno, y la mayoría abrumadora que ha perdido el ejercicio parcial o total de sus derechos o bienes, por la otra.

c. Los integrantes del gobierno, sus familiares y amigos detentan todo el poder político, económico, militar y hasta el religioso de la nación.

d. No existe división de poderes, sino solo en sentid o formal.

e. No existe renovación periódica de autoridades, o lo es entre el mismo círculo reducido de individuos.

f. Todo lo decide el Poder Ejecutivo (rey, presidente, primer ministro).

g. No se respetan los derechos y garantías constitucionales.

h. Se suprime a la oposición política.

i. Las leyes se promulgan y se aplican sin respetar a la Constitución.

j. Existe un descreimiento generalizado de la población en sus gobernantes.

k. La política y la administración civil pierde n legitimidad.

l. La carga impositiva y arancelaria recae con exclusividad en los sectores carentes de privilegio.

m. El soborno es una práctica extendida entre todos los sectores de la población. Nada puede conseguirse sin un pago ilegal previo.

n. Contribuye a generar violencia regional, étnica y religiosa.

o. Disminuye el nivel de vida de la sociedad.

p. Encarece el costo burocrático y reduce su eficiencia.

q. Prima el nepotismo y el caudillismo en toda la administración.

r. Frustra a los funcionarios competentes y honestos que terminan perdiendo sus cargos.

s. Subvierte toda forma de cooperación o confianza.

t. Inhibe cualquier intento de innovación o reforma.

u. El delito se generaliza y se vuelve incontrolable.

v.   Cunde la inseguridad política e individual."

4.1 — Juridical Nihilism and Disbelief in the State

It is seen that corruption brings with it legal nihilism involving the individual and the public official in a destructive association of the foundations of the democratic state.

Corruption solidifies the disbelief in the State's ability to respond efficiently and effectively to the demands for social well-being that are proposed to it, as Héctor A. Mairal (2007: 42-43) points out:

"La inseguridad jurídica que venimos de describir tiene como consecuencia colocar en situación de indefensión tanto al ciudadano en general como al mismo funcionario público. En ambos casos, esa situación favorece el desarrollo de la corrupción, amén de tener graves consecuencias para la vida cívica del país. Si, como bien se ha dicho, la existencia del Estado de Derecho depende, entre otras condiciones, de que las normas jurídicas sean estables, públicas y lo más definidas que sea posible, cabra concluir que la Argentina aun dista de ser un verdadero Estado de Derecho. ( )

La indefensión de los particulares tiene un efecto adiciona aunque indirecto, sobre la corrupción, al desalentar las críticas a los funcionarios públicos cuando están en la cumbre de su poder por temor a sus represalias; La indefensión crea temor y el temor de los ciudadanos es un buen aliado de la impunidad de los poderosos. El resultado es que la critica a la corrupción - tema hoy inevitable en el discurso social y político - es esporádica y tímida frente a los poder - habientes, pero - como contrapartida - es constante, despiadada y no siempre justa hacia quienes ya no lo poseen. Y como muchos de quienes critican no se preocupan tanto por llegar a la verdad respecto de los verdaderos casos de corrupción, sino que, al amparo de la natural morosidad de los trámites judiciales, en realidad buscan destruir políticamente a los adversarios, la conclusión que la clase política extrae de este fenómeno es que el recado radica en la pérdida del poder y no en la práctica de la corrupción. De allí la tendencia a modificar la Constitución para permitir la reelección que se ha observado tanto a nivel nacional como provincial. Cincinato no es un modelo para los políticos argentinos."

The harmful consequences of acts of corruption affect man as a whole and are directly related to the dispute over power, which is why they inhibit the capacity for development and undermine the educational process that forms the ethical man.

There are those who argue that a bit of corruption helps in the development of countries and people because without it public policies in some continents, such as the African, for example, are not implemented.

It is necessary to be careful with such ideas, because as Marilena Chauí says (1988: 92) *"Ideology is the process by which the ideas of the ruling class become ideas of all social classes, becoming, therefore, dominant ideas."*

The current democratic state has long been unable to justify its neglect with the indignity to which most of its citizens were relegated, despite having the human and material resources to provide a substantial democracy, rather than this formal democracy in which we live.

There is an endless number of studies that teach how to govern, and manuals that teach how to exercise control over *res publicae*, so the excuses for not knowing what to do are no longer valid. Jean Claude Thoenig and Yves Meny (1992: 181) assert that:

"Una cosa es reunir informaciones y otra depurarlas y combinarlas entre ellas para permitir el análisis. Desde este punto de vista, se aconseja recurrir a procedimientos tales como:

- un pre análisis rápido, o sea, la confrontación «en caliente», a medida que avanza la encuesta, de los datos recogidos sobre lo que está sucediendo;

- la construcción de secuencias cronológicas, a condición de no encerrar el análisis ulterior en una sola perspectiva histórica y lineal, reducida a los acontecimientos, de los efectos de causalidad;
- la confrontación sistemática sobre un mismo sujeto de las informaciones provenientes de varias fuentes, no tanto para separar lo venadero de lo falso, cuanto para descubrir las racionalidades particulares en acción."

We understand that we cannot close our eyes to the reality that corruption exists and that it reaches some achievements, but we believe that corruption must always be analyzed under the prism of ethics. It is like a heavy drug: its side effects will appear and they will lead the patient to death.

In the study on corruption, economic development and ethics look at each other suspiciously. What factor contributes the most to reducing corruption: economic development or social equality?

Manuel Villoria Mendieta, when studying *Ética pública y corrupción* (2000: 104,106) states that:

"En principio, del análisis del «índice de percepción de corrupción», de *Transparency International*, se podría deducir que el desarrollo económico es un factor a considerar, pero no el más importante; así, masque desarrollo económico es la existencia de un avanzado estado de bienestar lo que reduce las posibilidades de corrupción. (...)

La desigualdad genera incertidumbre por cuatro razones: en primer lugar, los tratos son realizados entre actores con capacidades muy diferentes de negociación, por lo que la percepción de inequidad es posible que se produzca y generalice; segundo, la inequidad percibida induce al engaño y los comportamientos oportunistas, pues el trato deja de ser justo y moralmente sostenible; tercero, la capacidad de manipulación de los mecanismos regulatorios y de justicia, por parte de los más ricos, obliga a minimizar riesgos para caso de incumplimiento, con lo que no se extraen todas las posibilidades de mutua ventaja del acuerdo; cuarto, la información con la que cuentan los más poderosos es muy superior a la del resto, sus contactos en la Administración y sus posibilidades de usar información privilegiada son elevados, con lo que los intercambios se realizan en situación de desigualdad con el resto de actores, por lo que estos tenderán a evitar la transacción o a minimizar sus riesgos.

En una sociedad desigual, sobre todo si no existen unos servicios sociales avanzados, el trato entre los ciudadanos para el disfrute de los bienes colectivos es inequitativo, pues los más ricos disfrutan mucho más de los bienes comunes, como aeropuertos, carreteras, cultura, seguridad pública. Además, su relación con la justicia se realiza en términos de inequidad, pues pueden pagar caros abogados, dilatar el proceso e, incluso, influenciar a los jueces. Finalmente, su capacidad de relacionarse con el poder político y de financiar partidos provoca que obtengan regulaciones que favorecen su posición de mercado. Los más ricos, en consecuencia, pueden actuar con tendencias monopolísticas u oligopolísticas, incrementando la posibilidad de comportamientos oportunistas."

4.2 – Social Inequality and Disbelief in National Institutions

Inequality generates uncertainties and generalizes iniquity, multiplies opportunistic behaviors, and broadens the manipulative capacity of the rich over regulatory means and justice. Finally, says Mendieta, the information that the rich hold always allows them to minimize their risks in relation to the rest of the population.

4.3 – Nine other consequences of corruption

In addition to the harmful consequences cited by Mendieta, corruption breaks down one of the main socio-political assets of the State protected by the law, which is public trust in its institutions, according to Cincunegui (1996: 28,30):

> "La 'confianza pública' debe ser uno de los bienes sociopolíticos principales tutelados por la ley. En efecto, de la realización de actividades o tareas publicas y el ejercicio de funciones o potestades publicas - en todos los niveles - depende en gran medida la 'confianza pública', especialmente respecto a aquellos que deben interpretar, administrar, aplicar y ejecutar las leyes que regulan las actividades a su cargo. La actuación de los mismos debe ser objetiva y servir al interés público. (...)
> La corrupción tiene consecuencias que trascienden los efectos de la transacción corrupta:

- Quiebra de la fe y la confianza pública en sus gobernantes y resquebrajamiento de la vigencia del Estado de Derecho, del sistema democrático.
- Debilitamiento del cuerpo social como carburante del cambio y la evolución político-social, en razón de que nadie piensa que con el voto del electorado podrán suprimirse los elementos indeseados de las situaciones sociales.
- Perdida de incentivos de la ciudadanía por las cosas públicas, desprestigio de constituirse en político, creación de una casta o clase (la de los políticos) a la que se señala como privilegiada, sea o no del partido gobernante, y que esta llamada para lograr beneficios propios o de sus familiares o amigos. No existe en la sociedad carcomida por la corrupción sensación de que los políticos representan al pueblo y que su objetivo es el bien común.
- Destrucción de valores sociales y del sistema de meritos e incentivos, basados en la corrección, la virtud, y la justa conducta de los ciudadanos.

A medida en que la corrupción se generaliza y los corruptores y corruptos no son perseguidos y castigados, ni se les aplica la sanción social, los demás ciudadanos si no tienen valores éticos muy fuertes y arraigados, se ven impelidos a acometer conductas similares o, en su defecto, padecer los efectos de la exclusión social, siendo señalados como perdedores en medio de una sociedad utilitarista y competitiva.

- En una sociedad ampliamente penetrada por la corrupción, incluso las personas honestas, si quieren seguir trabajando, deber inclinarse ante las exigencias de los corruptos para poder desenvolverse normalmente. Podríamos citar decenas de ejemplos demostrativos de esta forma de sojuzgar conciencias.
- Distorsión de los procesos democráticos de selección de gobernantes, a través del logro de lealtades atadas a las contribuciones económicas para las internas y para las elecciones generales.
- A través de la justicia, cuando la misma no es independiente, se logra la impunidad de los actos corruptos y además la persecución de los enemigos, a través de procesos dirigidos, inventados, etc. que duran años y que proscriben a quienes molestan el camino de la toma o retención del poder.
- Los sistemas corruptos expulsan a los funcionarios honrados.
- Producen distorsiones en las economías de mercado y enormes beneficios en negro que distraen del Tesoro Público o de los contribuyentes y usuarios de los servicios públicos, que por supuesto no entran dentro del circuito económico, sino que son desviados a paraísos fiscales o se mantienen resguardados para ser utilizados en la acumulación de más poder."

Summarizing what Cincunegui said, corruption:

1 - Breaks the faith and public trust in the democratic system;
2 - Weakens the society since it starts to discredit that its vote can be an inducer of changes in the political system;
3 - Generates the creation of privileged political castes to the detriment of the situation of the people;
4 - Destroys the social values of virtue;
5 - Expels honest officials.

Dr. Horst Schónbohm of the *Asociacion de magistrados del Uruguay* (1998: 31), in a speech dated April 1998 in Montevideo, addressing *"El poder judicial frente a la corrupción"* says that corruption:

> "socava la democracia y los principios de legalidad, además de afectar negativamente al derecho constitucional de la igualdad, viola los principios de la justicia social, lesiona el interés común, impide el progreso y termina por destruir el consenso básico de la sociedad y afecta negativamente a la gobernabilidad, fomenta el rentismo, lesiona los principios de la justicia social y afecta al régimen de competencia en una economía de mercado, causa importantes daños económicos."

Horst (32-33) also shows the following characteristics of corruption processes:

> "interviene más de una persona, se crea una relación de mutuo beneficio y obligación, ocultamiento sistemático del accionar, se concreta entre quienes influyen el as decisiones y quienes pueden influir sobre estas, se incurre siempre en un abuso de confianza, se mezclan decisiones públicas con decisiones empresarias o particulares, los intervinientes vulneran los deberes y las responsabilidades."

This chapter cannot be concluded without the reflection of Guillermo Ariel Todarello (2008: 176-177), when he affirms that corruption schemes denaturalize the State. His refection is stellar:

> "El desarrollo de esquemas de corrupción estructural dentro del ámbito de la administración pública deriva indefectiblemente en la desnaturalización del Estado. Ello así por cuanto, en lugar de conformar una estructura organizada y destinada al cumplimiento de sus funciones básicas - las cuales se hallan relacionadas con la búsqueda de elementos que coadyuven al bienestar general - y de proveer el marco adecuado para posibilitar el desarrollo de cada uno de los ciudadanos, se convierte

gradualmente en una organización que produce en cambio el ambiente y los recursos apropiados para la realización de actos irregulares y, eventualmente, delictivos. Dicha transformación desemboca definitivamente en una situación de debilitamiento institucional, circunstancia que impido a toda nación alcanzar un nivel sustentable de desarrollo."

4.4 – The Privatization of Law

We can also say that corruption privatizes the law because it makes it hostage to those who, in the name of economic interests, focus on income, increasing levels of inequality and exposing the incapacity of the modern state.

It seems correct to say that one of the most damaging consequences of corruption is the emergence of blood crimes and, subsequently, the emergence of economic crimes. Todarello (2008: 91) perceived this reflection from the work of Montesquieau and Jean Jeacques Rousseau, reason why Todarello affirmed:

> "Al igual que lo expuesto por los anteriores filósofos (v. gr., Montesquieu), Rousseau también destaca la importancia de gobernar ejemplificativamente y sin recurrir a hechos de corrupción; ello como medio o instrumento para prevenir la mayor cantidad de delitos posibles que puedan provocarse en el marco de dicho estado vicioso (o al menos evitar la impunidad de sus autores); subrayando también la inconveniencia de pretender corregir dichas conductas con la mera aplicación y endurecimiento de sanciones, lo cual constituye, en definitiva, un signo de mal gobierno. Por ello, esgrime: "En un Estado bien gobernado hay pocas penas, no porque se otorgan muchos perdones, sino por existir pocos criminales. Solo el decaimiento del Estado es decir, su inmersión en un estado de corrupción asegura la impunidad a multitud de crímenes"

Socrates said that the "state of corruption" leads the State to bankruptcy. Ancient philosophers pledged to rule by example. Governments have been doing the opposite and proving that the law has much more relative value than we thought it had.

In the current moment of globalization of information it is possible to believe that a new Enlightenment is about to occur because never in the history of mankind has man known so much about himself.

Innocence is becoming obsolete, and the subjugated ones do not fully conform to the frame of Rousseau's old "The Social Contract". It is already possible to notice a certain shaking in social structure.

We believe that the Right of Resistance established in the Virginia Declaration of Rights will occupy its place in time and space, as said by Professor David S. Landes:

> "...wealth is an irresistible magnet; and poverty is a potentially vile agent of contamination; cannot be segregated, and our peace and prosperity depend, in the long run, on the well-being of others."

CHAPTER 5

The Profile of the Corrupt

Tracing a person's profile is the task of psychology or psychiatry. Sigmund Schlomo Freud analyzing *"El delincuente por sentimiento de culpabilidad"* offers us arguments to believe that the good man and the evil man can be the same person.

This is how Freud (1968: 1093) outlines his thinking:

> "En sus informes sobre sus años juveniles, especialmente sobre los anteriores a la pubertad, personas honradísimas luego y de elevada moralidad me han revelado, frecuentemente, haber cometido por entonces actos ilícitos, tales como hurtos, fraudes e incluso incendios. En un principio solía yo dejar de lado estos hechos, explicando-los por la conocida debilidad de las inhibiciones morales en aquella época de la vida, y no intentaba insértalos en un más amplio contexto. Pero el examen de algunos casos más claros y favorables, en los que tales actos fueran cometidos por enfermos míos durante el tratamiento y en edad muy posterior a aquellos años juveniles, me impulsó ya a un estudio más penetrante y detenido de estos incidentes. La labor analítica me condujo entonces al sorprendente resultado de que tales actos eran cometidos, ante todo, porque se hallaban prohibidos y porque a su ejecución se enlazaba, para su autor, en un alivio psíquico. EL sujeto sufría, se efecto, de un penoso

sentimiento de culpabilidad, de origen desconocido, y una vez cometida una falta concreta sentía mitigada la presión del mismo. El sentimiento de culpabilidad quedaba así, por lo menos, adherido a algo tangible."

5.1 — Homo Sapiens is Corrupt

We may say to say the corrupt has the profile of whomever is poor, rich, creative, inventive, intelligent, wise, religious, atheist, leader, or subservient. In short, the corrupt is a human being like any other because to corrupt and to allow himself to be corrupted all needed is to be "man" and live in society.

David S. Landes (1998: 38-39,45) saw corruption in this profile of the common man and described it as follows:

> "The contest for power in European societies (note the plural) also gave rise to the specifically European phenomenon of the semi-autonomous city, organized and known as commune. (...) The consequences were felt throughout the society. Under this special dispensation, cities became poles of attraction, places of refuge, and nodes of exchange with the countryside. Migration to cities improved the income and status not only of the migrants but of those left behind. (But not their health. The cities were dirty, crowded, and lent themselves to easy contagion, so that it was only in-migration that sustained their numbers and enabled them to grow.) (...)
>
> Why did rulers grant such rights to rustics and townsmen, in effect abandoning (transferring) some of their own powers? Two reasons above all. First, new land, new crops, trade, and markets brought revenue, and revenue brought power. (Also pleasure.) Second, paradoxically, rulers wanted to enhance their power within their own kingdom: free farmers (note that I do not say "peasants") and townsmen (bourgeois) were the natural enemies of the

landed aristocracy and would support the crown and other great lords in their struggles with local seigneurs. (…)

Besides, the urban setting itself made it necessary to ration space and time, again with an eye to discouraging self-aggrandizement. So, no stealing a march and selling before a certain hour or after another; no price competition; no trade-off of quality and solidity for cheapness; no buying low ("jewing down," in popular parlance—bad habits always belong to someone else) to sell high; in short, no market competition. Everyone who did his job was entitled to a living. Laudable but static. The aim was an egalitarian social justice, but it entailed serious constraint on enterprise and growth—a safety net at the expense of income.

That was the principle. One should always assume that rules, then as now, were made to be broken."

Of all the men who inhabit the planet, the "religious man" is the one who most pretends to hold an incorruptible profile, but the historical word that best described them and still describes 99% of them is that said by Jesus in Matthew 23:27: *Woe to you, scribes and Pharisees, hypocrites! For you are like whitewashed tombs, which indeed appear beautiful outwardly, but inside are full of dead men's bones and all uncleanness.*

History is full of bad legacies of all religions, and, to illustrate such truth, we repeat what Professor David Landes (1998: 37) said:

"Yet Western medieval Christianity did come to condemn the pretensions of earthly rulers—lesser monarchs, to be sure, than the emperors of Rome. (The Eastern Church never talked back to the Caesars of Byzantium.) It thereby implicitly gave protection to private property. As the Church's own claims to power increased, it could not but emphasize the older Judaic principle that the real owner of everything was the Lord above, and the newer Christian principle that the pope was his vicar here below. Earthly rulers were not free to do as they pleased, and even the Church, God's surrogate on

> earth, could not flout rights and take at will. The elaborate paperwork that accompanied the transfer of gifts of the faithful bore witness to this duty of good practice and proper procedure."

Christianity, in its more than 2000 years, was introduced as an inclusive religion of those who believe and are baptized, but excluding those who do not accept its dogmas. This religion has gone through innumerable phases, including tolerance and, in the hands of utilitarian religious, has become extremely intolerant.

It cannot be denied that Christianity is more democratic than some other religions. However, the so-called faith introduced by Jesus who said, *"if you want to be perfect, go, sell your possessions and give to the poor"* was substituted by a new preaching of pastors, missionaries, and bishops, for whom what is imperative is the theory of *come all, including you who are poor, and give all you have so that I can travel by private jet, finance my companies, and sustain my life of opulence!*

Corruption also clung to religion. This is why, in this work, we are not naïve to proclaim the extinction of corruption. The message we want to be assimilated is that we have full ethical, moral, and legal conditions to reduce it to tolerable levels, and, if we do so, we can substantiate this formal democracy that explicitly promises yet denies the minimum welfare due to every citizen.

In April 2010 in Lisbon, Portugal, magistrates, sociologists, lawyers, and politicians debated corruption with the intention of developing a study in partnership between the Central Department of Investigation and Criminal Action (DCIAP) and the Center for Research and Sociology Studies of the Superior Institute of Business and Labor Sciences (CIES-ISCTE).

At the time, the sociologist Luís de Sousa said that *"the corruptor has the profile of the common citizen"* and that crime can only be fought *"if there is no longer a culture of complacency in society."*

Being corruption a substratum of conscious and free life and man the recipient of this greater good, we conclude that corruption does not depart from virtue of religion, economy, ethics, morals, law, or any other domain of reason. A man can have the noblest feelings and still corrupt or allow himself to be corrupted by will or necessity.

It is even possible that a person corrupts himself unintentionally, that is, when the fact is committed under coercion or in strict obedience to an order, not necessarily illegal, of a hierarchical superior, a hypothesis in which justice and law recommend punishment only to the author of coercion.

Plinio de Arruda Sampaio (2009: 5-6), in his paper *How to Fight Corruption*, holds harmless those who act under duress they could not resist. This is what he says:

> "But at this point, it is important to clarify: not every person who bribes is corrupt. It depends on the possibility that this person has to resist the proposal of the corruptor. If the refusal to give the required bribe causes serious harm to the person, he is more in the position of a victim than of a corrupt person."

Friedrich Nietzsche in his work *"La genealogía de la moral"* (2007: 17) debates on the profile of the moral man ensuring that there is no doubt that the "good man" overcomes the "evil man" in value matters and adds to the reasoning issues that are true warnings:

> "que esta superioridad del valor resulta tal, en el sentido de ser algo propicio, útil, ventajoso para el hombre como tal (incluido el futuro del hombre). ¿Qué ocurriría si la verdad fuera precisamente al revés? ¿Qué ocurriría si el hombre 'bueno' estuviera afectado también por un síntoma de retroceso y, asimismo, un peligro, una seducción, un veneno, una especie de narcótico, y que a raíz de esto el presente viviese tal vez á expensas del futuro? ¿Se viviría quizá de manera más confortable, menos peligrosa, pero también con un estilo inferior y de un modo más bajo?"

It is not easy to answer Nietzsche's question about what would happen if the evil man dominated, but I do not think the question is completely unanswered because every day we witness the consequences of evil and corruption.

Is corruption a crime? Is corruption a sign of violence? The answer to these two questions can be both objective and subjective. Objectively, we can say that it will be a crime whenever society typifies such conduct. Subjectively, it will be a form of violence whenever the conduct is intended to harm others' rights, following the Hobbesian orientation of *Quod tibi fieri non vis, alteri ne feceris* or "do unto others as you would have them do unto you."

CHAPTER 6

The Allies of Corruption

Corruption is an idea that is embodied in the conduct of a conscious and free man and that implies a deviation from the ethical character that the social educational process aims to relegate as a cultural heritage.

Since corruption is not an entity, but a conduct that is personified in the conscious and free man, this action is strengthened insofar as social circumstances are favorable to it. We will refer to these circumstances favorable to corruption as allies.

An ally is the one or that which makes an alliance or connection with something or someone. We present the following allies of corruption:

1 - evil human nature and religion;
2 - the law;
3 - discretion;
4 - juridical nihilism;
5 - the ambiguity of the norms, their dubious validity and other
      wrongdoings of the State;
6 - State Disregard of the Law.

6.1 – Evil Human Nature and Religion

There are many allies of corruption. One of them is the evil human nature that spreads throughout all fields of life, including religion, which should be a source of redemption for the excluded. Harrison Oliveira (1984: 27) reports the following experience:

"One a given day, I ran to the priest's house to receive his blessings (old habit mania from a provincial boy). At the waiting room, I was confronted with a very interesting, but very surreal scene: the parish priest of the city, Monsignor Jose Delgado (now Bishop of the State of Maranhão) was helping an entire family of a miserable countryman. They were, in all, five children, the husband, the wife, and a stray dog. While waiting for the blessing from Father Delgado, I heard the following dialogue:

-Dear Father, I need some help for my family. I'm out of work and I'm starving!

-The alms, my son, are already finished because they have already been distributed with the first ones who requested them. Come on another occasion and you will be helped.

-But Dear Father, I'm tired of asking around, going through the streets. I went to the City Hall, to stores, and the answers are always the same. We are starving and suffering a lot!

Monsignor Delgado, with that round, pale, and nourished, shaped like a full moon face, adjusted his tortoise-rimmed glasses on his nose, and in a cavernous voice replied:

- Suffer, my children, for Christ also suffered for us on the cross "Blessed are those who hunger and thirst for theirs is the Kingdom of Heaven"!

Having said that, the priest took the rosary, separated the crucifix from the beads, and gave it for the whole family to kiss. He said goodbye promising a good after life for the visitors."

At the time of the Lutheran Reform, the Church and the State, once separated, had once again merged.

It was necessary for Luther to break with ninety-five papal dogmas in his parish, in Wittemberg, so that an almost insignificant reform would create a cover up that would leave the Church a little more like "the bride of Christ" than the "bride of the State".

At that time the *sacerdotum* was the owner of the wealth that flowed in the Western world, reason why one of its most common practices was to encourage the faithful to make a vow of poverty for the church to inherit their possessions.

Undoubtedly, separating State and Church, two powerful forces and desirous of power, is not an easy task. Quentin Skinner (1996: 341-342) historically addressing the rupture between *regnum* and *sacerdotum* says:

"In Denmark the danger-level was reached under Christian II, with his promulgation in 1521-2 of the Byretten Civil and Ecclesiastical Code. This proposed to end all Appeals to Rome (...)"

This separation to this day has not been completely taken place and, judging by the practices of modern Christianity, the exploration of the *sacerdotum* over the people has only been disguised. Nevertheless, in essence, the forgiveness of sins continues to be sold at the expense of the new indulgences charged by the churches in which theological doctrine gave way to the economic appeal without the slightest ethical or moral decency. The Christian clergy are, again, blatantly thriving at the expense of blind faith.

Priests, pastors, bishops, and missionaries have already discovered that religion is a channel through which wealth flows, with almost no supervision of the State. This circumstance allows any kind of corruption in the name of God, including money laundering, and creation of structures of psychological domination in which personal and family dogma reigns over the cells of rich, poor, and miserable people waiting to implant the kingdom of God on earth with the power of tithes, offerings, and other "witchcraft" that Christians have so fought over time.

Perhaps this is why Jesus said: *And because lawlessness will abound, the love of many will grow cold. (Mt. 24-12).*

Those who thus acted and continued acting led Friederich Nietzsche to say that God is dead:

"this old saint has not heard in his forest that God is dead!" (Thus Spoke Zarathustra)

Religion and its system of corruption killed God.

6.2 – Law

Ernesto Palacio (1998:69) said that *Los vicios de un pueblo son los de su clase dirigente.*

Is it possible that the State itself is an ally of corruption? Is it possible that economics, law, and democracy are allied with this human phenomenon?

Héctor A. Mairal (2007: 21) in his work *"Las raíces legales de la corrupción"* mentions ten circumstances that turn the Law an ally of corruption:

> "Para entender cómo opera el derecho en pro de la corrupción partimos de la premisa que una persona normal, enfrentada a un requerimiento claro y razonable de la norma, cuya violación es controlada y sancionada seriamente, preferirá cumplirla antes de arriesgar la sanción. Los argentinos no somos una excepción. Obsérvese, si no, el comportamiento mayoritario de nuestros compatriotas cuando habitan en países cuyos sistemas jurídicos siguen esas pautas.
>
> Ciertas características de un sistema jurídico, sin embargo, pueden llegar a cambiar esa preferencia en un determinado porcentaje de casos o, aun sin cambiarla, a colocar a las personas en situación de incumplimiento sancionable pese a intentar cumplir con la norma o creer que lo están haciendo. Así ocurre con el derecho argentino debido a las siguientes características que presenta:

> • La misma existencia de la norma suele ser desconocida para gran parte de las personas que debieran cumplirla.
> • Debido a los continuos cambios normativos es difícil saber a ciencia cierta cuál es el texto vigente de la norma aplicable.
> • Las normas suelen ser oscuras y admitir diversas interpretaciones, algunas de las cuales elevan, y otras reducen, considerablemente el costo de su cumplimiento.
> • Las normas son frecuentemente de validez dudosa.

- De hecho o de derecho, las normas suelen permitir al funcionario determinar el grado de cumplimiento que cabe exigir a cada particular o a cada categoría de ellos.
- Muchas veces es difícil o imposible cumplir cabalmente con la norma, o costo de cumplimiento es muy elevado, pone en riesgo la continuidad de la conducta privada o, lisa y llanamente, la impide.
- El control suele ser laxo por lo cual la probabilidad de la detección del incumplimiento es muy reducida.
- Aun sin ser laxo el control, la autoridad suele permitir el funcionamiento de un sector de la sociedad en violación de la norma y sanciona a un porcentaje reducido de incumplidores, a quienes selecciona no siempre con criterios transparentes y políticamente neutrales.
- En algunos casos (como ocurre en materia ambiental) es más barato afrontar las multas que llevar a cabo las tareas que impone la ley.
- Aunque el castigo previsto sea muy grave, las ventajas derivadas del incumplimiento de la norma generalmente son tan elevadas que justifican correr el riesgo de detección."

Society is not a legal construction. Theologically, it is a divine construction. Anthropologically speaking, it is both biological and political constructions because it comes from bacteria, and also because it is made up of political animals, respectively.

Thus, it seems well that every science and every institute derived from it should be evaluated within its context. Law, however, seems to be the science that attempts to harmonize society, amalgamating its multiple understandings in order to avoid conflict.

Some scholars in the field of law see the subject as the science that formulates rules for peaceful existence in society. There are even those who defend their supremacy over politics.

Karl Marx and Friedrich Engels preach differently because they understand that economy conditions life in society.

A fact inseparable from history is that Law has always been an instrument of dominance. Its laws have always served to the powerful as a means of controlling the lower classes, under the promise of equality.

Throughout history, legislators took prominent roles in governments, under the guise of the laws being the works of the "divine". Therefore, the lawmakers would be those chosen and deserving of "worship" and the benefits of State power.

Time has passed. Enlightenment displaced God from its central position, and man took his rightful place on the planet. Among powerful men, jurists stood out until the late seventies of the twentieth century.

This dispute over political power among economists, jurists, philosophers, and other categories ended up engendering the professional politician for whom the mandate is a means of producing his personal interest or that of whom is financing him.

The diagram presented below depicts the dispute between law, economics, and politics, emphasizing that whereas jurists think that power is with the Law, economists like Marx and Engels argue that the economy is what conditions the government.

As we see it, both law and economy are servants of the modern political class, who do not seek the supreme well being, yet are content to subdue the State and its entire structure to its personal interests.

Here are the three conceptions about the influence of law, economy, and politics on the government.

1 - LEGAL CONCEPTION: defended by the actors of the law:

LEGAL SPHERE

(the safe management of a State lies in the
hands of those who understand laws)

POLITICAL SPHERE

(makes laws according to the "spirit" of natural law – jusnaturalism - or according to the law of good human reasoning – Comte's positivism)

OTHER SCIENCES

(have added value to the development they help to promote, without being seen as an ideological threat)

According to dialectics, the economists reanalyzed the question and, when they realized that the possession of wealth is what determines who commands and who obeys, they revisited the dominance of science and enthroned economy over the other sciences. Here is a formula that represents this idea:

2 – ECONOMIC SCIENCE CONCEPTION: defended by Karl Marx and Friedrich Engels, German philosophers and economists, creators of communism:

ECONOMIC SPHERE

(the phenomena that drive life are the economic relations and, above all, the control of the means of production of a community)

POLITICAL SPHERE

(is the human field in which the agent will or will not make the fair distribution of wealth by balancing the means of production and the needs of the citizen)

LEGAL SPHERE

(represents a simple defense mechanism of the system of production which, in capitalism, is an "instrument of evil")

OTHER SCIENCES OR ARTS

(may pose a threat to the State if they are not ideologically useful to it)

Indeed, we understand that politics is the utmost science in the governance of life. Politics creates the rules that shape the character of government and society, for better or for worse.

We believe that the dominance of politics over other sciences is absolute, and that "political will" is the most important element of social acts and facts.

History is rich with examples of dominance. Below is what we believe to be the most appropriate formula of political dominance:

3 - POLITICAL DOMINANCE CONCEPTION

POLITICAL SPHERE

(power focuses on regimen of exception or is expressed in
legislative, judicial, and executive functions in democratic
societies, choosing useful accomplices for government activity)

LEGAL SPHERE

(is, in formal democracies, a mere useful tool for political actors.
Its byproducts, such as laws, doctrine, and jurisprudence are
means for purposes previously delimited by those in power)

OTHER SCIENCES

(are important and subject to investment spikes when their
product is useful to the dominant political class)

It is impossible to deny that the perspective of Law offered here diminishes its importance. This is not our intention, which is why it is time to think about a new model because the current the democratic State is bankrupt.

The increasing inequality between the political will that privileges a few and denies the minimum of social welfare to the most needy part of the population reflects the full denial of the justice preached by law.

6.3 - Discretion

In law, discretion is a judgment of opportunity and convenience of practicing a legal act. It is a power or administrative activity that, while privileging the balance among the executive, legislative and judicial branches, also creates numerous situations that enable acts and systems of corruption.

For example, when ordinary law relegates the regulation of rights and duties to certain public officials, they may use their own time as an ally to extort the recipient of rights.

The longer it takes to produce a legal act that creates or extinguishes rights, the more benefited agents become active and passive actors of corruption.

Discretion allows imposing the obstacle, creating the difficulty for the employee to bargain for the "facility" that only those who can afford have access to it. It is this employee who, exercising police power, notifies or not the illegality liable to fine or suspends public and private undertakings.

It is this same employee who, in the judgment of opportunity and convenience, fictitiously diminishes the footage of the constructed area of the land to increase or decrease property tax. He is also the one who plants evidence to extort the innocent citizen and it is he who eliminates the evidence of his guilt, all because he has in hand the backup of the law that enables him to act with discretion, that is, in the judgment of what is most favorable and convenient.

We do not defend the extermination of discretion. This is not the case! What we are saying is that the instruments of control not only have to exist, but, above all, to be effective because the sanction to the offender must take into account that those who do not infringe, may not infringe because they covet little, but because they have little power to take advantage of their position, function, job, or public term.

Discretion is a strong ally of corruption, as Mairal (2007: 22) states:

> "A su vez, la discrecionalidad del funcionario público argentino responsable de controlar y sancionar el incumplimiento es muy grande debido a la presencia de los siguientes factores adicionales:
>
> • No siempre es posible, para los particulares, obtener la oportuna intervención judicial para confirmar el sentido o la validez de la norma sin correr el riesgo de ser sancionados por su incumplimiento.
> • La sanción suele ser de tal gravedad que puede llevar a la prisión o a la quiebra del incumplidor.
> • El control administrativo sobre el funcionario sancionador es escaso. Más aun, la sanción está bien vista, aunque sea injusta, ya que ella exime al funcionario de sospechas de parcialidad.

- El control judicial sobre la decisión del funcionario es ineficaz, por lento, costoso o por la existencia de doctrinas jurídicas que permiten predecir una decisión contraria al particular."

6.4 - Legal Nihilism

The list of allies of corruption is self-explanatory and shocking. Hector Mairal (2007: 23) also asserts that legal nihilism is allied with corruption. Here is how he teaches it:

> "Que la inseguridad jurídica actúa como aliada de la corrupción no es, ciertamente, un fenómeno novedoso. Un autor que ha estudiado la corrupción como causa d la decadencia del imperio romano enumera ciertos factores que en aquella lejana época favorecían la corrupción al facilitar la extorsión de los articulares por los funcionarios públicos: El creciente grado de violencia empleado por el Gobierno hacia los particulares, la ambigüedad, de las leyes, aumento de su número y el carácter intrusivo de las normas y de los funcionarios. Estos mismos factores, todos ellos causantes de inseguridad jurídica e indirectamente de corrupción, se encuentran presentes hoy día en nuestro país."

The principle of legal certainty is foreseen, for example, in Article 5 of the Brazilian Constitution of 1988, in the following terms:

> "XXXVI - no law may impair a vested right, a perfected juristic act or *res judicata*;"

The Democratic State must protect its own law. For this reason, it tries to curb losses to the vested right, to the perfected juristic act, and the *res judicata*, in a way to end respect to the law.

Resolution 456, of October 15, 2013, which contains the veto of the President of the Federative Republic of Brazil to Bill 40 of 2013, is a good element of interpretation of the meaning of the principle of legal certainty, which is why it is here transcribed:

"Dear President of the Senate,

I hereby inform you that, pursuant to § 1 of Article 66 of the Constitution, decided to partially veto, in opposition to the public interest and unconstitutionality, Bill Number 40, of 2013 (Number 4,280/08 in the House of Representatives), which addresses the exercise of the activity and the remuneration of the lottery's permittee and provides other measures.

After being consulted, the Secretary of Finance and Planning, Budget, and Management expressed their veto to the following:

Article 3, Subsection IV:

IV - the price of bets must be updated annually by an official economic index to be defined by the Finance Committee of the Department of Treasury, always having as base of calculation the price established at the date of creation of each type of lottery;

Reasons for veto:

The value of bets on lotteries should be defined in terms of demand for the service and, above all, public policy objectives. In addition, by requiring the annual price adjustment according to the economic index would eventually generate a pressure for readjustment and would unduly contribute to inflation.

The Secretary of Treasury and the Attorney-General of the Union opted for the veto of the following transcript:

Article 5, Subsection II:

II – will adopt the necessary measures to adapt the current contracts with the permittees and correspondents, waiving a new bidding, and the bidding processes or contracts in progress, prevailing the rules of this Law on the revising rules and other legal or administrative rules governing the instruments.

Reason for veto:

The act denies the principle of legal certainty in establishing that the rules of this law would prevail indiscriminately on the revising conditions and the rules established in existing contracts.

These, Mr. President, are the reasons that have led me to veto the aforementioned provisions of the bill in question, which I submit to the high appreciation of the Members of the National Congress.

This text does not replace the one published in the Brazilian National Archives of 10.16.2013."

One of the most favorable circumstances for corruption arises when the law is weakened by legal nihilism. If the State makes the *res judicata*, the perfected juristic act, or the vested right a vulnerable circumstance, it demonstrates that it does not respect itself since its essence is that of a democratic State.

We understand that in such circumstances the people become holders of the right of resistance and can exercise it until it finds a government that provides the minimum welfare that the Liberal State promises.

Skinner (2006: 611) in dealing with the right of resistance points out:

"As Buchanan states, the people not only have the power to bestow the Empire upon their king, one should not even imagine that these people make a transmission

of their original sovereignty; what it does is to determine
to its king the form of the Empire."

6.5 - Ambiguity of the Norms, Their Dubious Validity and Other Wrongdoings of the State

Ambiguity refers to anything that carries more than one interpretation. Sometimes the ambiguity of the laws is deliberate because, in doubt, the lawyer already knows that the State will decide in favor of the defendant. This, we agree, does not always serve to social interests even if it serves the political-juridical interests.

In Brazil there is a law that teaches how to write laws. It is the Complementary Law 95/1998. Its Article13, Subsection VI recommends avoiding ambiguities. Here is an important excerpt:

> "Article 13. Federal laws will be unified in codifications and consolidations, composed of volumes containing related matters, constituting in its entirety the Consolidation of Federal Law. (With wording given by Complementary Law 107, of 04/26/2001)
>
> Paragraph 1. Consolidation shall consist of the integration of all laws relevant to a given matter into a single legal instrument, formally repealing the laws incorporated for consolidation, without changing the scope or interruption of the normative force of the consolidated provisions. (Paragraph added by Complementary Law 107, of 04/26/2001)
>
> Paragraph 2. Preserving the original normative content of the consolidated provisions, the following changes in the consolidation bills may be made: (Paragraph added by Complementary Law 107, of 04/26/2001)

I -   introduction of new divisions of the legal base text; (Paragraph added by Complementary Law 107, of 04/26/2001)

II -   different placement and numbering of the consolidated articles; (Paragraph added by Complementary Law 107, of 04/26/2001)

III - merging of repetitive provisions or of identical normative value; (Paragraph added by Complementary Law 107, of 04/26/2001)

IV -   updating the name of organs and entities of the public administration; (Paragraph added by Complementary Law 107, of 04/26/2001)

V -   updating dated terms and writing modes; (Paragraph added by Complementary Law 107, of 04/26/2001)

VI -   updating of the value of monetary penalties, based on standard indexing; (Paragraph added by Complementary Law 107, of 04/26/2001)

VII - eliminating ambiguities arising from the misuse of the vernacular; (Paragraph added by Complementary Law 107, of 04/26/2001)

VIII - terminological homogenization of the text; (Paragraph added by Complementary Law 107, of 04/26/2001)

IX -   suppression of provisions declared unconstitutional by the Federal Supreme Court, observing, as appropriate, the suspension by the Senate of execution of provision, according to Article 52, X, of the Federal Constitution; (Paragraph added by Complementary Law 107, of 04/26/2001)

X -   indicating of provision not accepted by the Federal Constitution; (Paragraph added by Complementary Law 107, of 04/26/2001)

XI -   express statement of revocation of provisions implicitly revoked by future laws. (Paragraph added by Complementary Law 107, of 04/26/2001)

Paragraph 3 - The measures referred to in items IX, X, and XI of Paragraph 2 shall be expressed and duly justified, with a precise indication of the sources of information that served as basis. (Paragraph added by Complementary Law 107, of 04/26/2001)."

A democratic State that has laws capable of producing equality and does not make them effective is not worthy of the people who have legitimized it. It must be replaced by a new form of governing.

Mairal, with whom we agree, identifies the following as allies of corruption:

1 - the obscurity and ambiguity of norms;
2 - the dubious validity of the norms; and
3 - the restriction of access to justice imposed on citizens against abuse of authority.

He also says that State violence is one of the greatest allies of corruption. In his own words (2007: 37-38):

> "Es sorprendente cómo el sistema legal argentino ha llegado a tratar igual o aún peor, en aspectos procesales, al acusado de una infracción impositiva que al imputado de un delito de homicidio o apoderamiento de fondos públicos. Cuando las sanciones eran muy distintas, podía comprenderse esta diferencia, pero cuando las sanciones son equiparables (un evasor puede ser condenado a diez años de cárcel y un homicida recibir solo ocho años) deben aplicarse idénticos principios garantistas. El contraste es aún más nítido en el caso de los delitos contra la administración pública, y por ello típicos de los funcionarios públicos que son tratados con benevolencia por el Código Penal: El cohecho, el tráfico de influencias, la malversación de caudales públicos, las exacciones ilegales, las negociaciones incompatibles con el ejercicio de funciones públicas y el enriquecimiento ilícito de funcionarios, son todos delitos que llevan pena mínima inferior a tres años e son, por ende, excarcelables y susceptibles de condena condicional. La evasión impositiva, por el contrario, recibe una pena mínima de tres años y medio cuando su monto supera el millón de pesos por año y por impuesto (monto que no se aumentó después de la devaluación de 2002), y por ende no sería excarcelable, lo que significa que el acusado debería estar

detenido mientras se decide si existió o no la evasión, lo que frecuentemente requiere complicado y debatibles análisis jurídicos y contables. Tampoco es excarcelable (por tener cuatro años de pena mínima) el delito culposo de manejo de dineros de un fondo de pensión que causa perjuicio al mismo. (Y en la volátil economía argentina ¿qué administrador de un fondo de pensión puede estar seguro de no ser pasible de una acusación tal?) Ello significa que para el derecho argentino es menos grave que un funcionario público se embolse diez millones de pesos de fondos estatales que un particular busque evitar pagar de su bolsillo un impuesto de un millón de pesos, o que otro particular sea negligente en el manejo de los dineros de un fondo de pensión. Estas diferencias no parecen compatibles con la garantía constitucional de la razonabilidad ni con nuestros antecedentes patrios. En una ciudad de hombres libres, decía el decreto sobre honores a los magistrados redactado por MARIANO MORENO en diciembre de 1810, 'el magistrado no se distingue de los demás sino porque hace observar las leyes, en las demás funciones de la sociedad es un ciudadano sin otras consideraciones que las que merezca por sus virtudes.' Y ya desde los proyectos de Constitución de 1813 se definía a la igualdad como la exigencia de que la ley 'sea ella perceptiva, penal o aflictiva,' sea igual para todos."

6.6 - State Disregard of the Law

There is no greater display of contempt for law than impunity. God may have been wrong with his creations, but He at least drove the devil out of paradise when he broke the rules of coexistence.

We, on the contrary, not only tolerate the corrupt, but also sometimes vote for him/her. All that is necessary is that the corrupt cries in front of the TV cameras promising that next time he/she will do better. The question is: are we more merciful than God?

Regis Fernandes de Oliveira in his book *Gastos Publicos* (2012) says:

"Therefore, when deciding public spending, it is imperative to know who wants to dominate who. If it is the political party X that is in control of power, it will allocate resources only and solely to those who are aligned with it. Eventually, it will be able to answer to specific situations, exclusively to justify the continuity of spending with those who are faithful to it. It is important that domination does not become evident. Physical violence is the greatest of all forms of violence. However, it can be practiced by disguise, that is, with a strong criticism of somebody or some company, delegitimizing it.

If the mayor of a certain municipality is aligned with the governor, it is evident that most of the resources will be destined to him. Of course you can not abandon the mayor of the opposing side because violence will be obvious. It is important, therefore, that some resources are also allocated to him, but in a smaller quantity."

In fact, what the former mayor, former congressman, and former judge, Régis Fernandes de Oliveira does, is a formal complaint. He who has ears to hear, let him hear!

Héctor Mairal (2007: 41) emphasizes the contempt of the State for the law as reprehensible conduct. Here is an excerpt from his reflection:

"En una conferencia MARIANO GRONDONA explicaba el fenómeno del Estado violador de la ley recurriendo a la distinción de RAWLS entre lo legal y lo bueno. Cuando la ley se opone a lo que le Estado argentino considera 'bueno' éste tiende a postergar la ley. De esta manera, en su defensa de lo que él entiende es el interés público, el Estado argentino sacrifica una y otra vez el Estado de Derecho. La legalidad cede frente a las conveniencias inmediatas del erario púbico. (Cuando no de la política.) Las ventajas institucionales que, a largo plazo, se derivan del respeto a la ley son consideradas un lujo que valoramos pero que no podemos permitirnos es esta situación de emergencia perpetua en que, como bien se ha dicho, vivimos."

Now, if our Constitutions in the Mercosur offer as a guarantee of the "social contract", of which we are all signatories, the promise that our citizenship and dignity is based on the Democratic State, in accordance with Article 1 of the Brazilian Federal Constitution, and the State implodes its own grounds despising the law, won't one of the sides have broken the contract? And when one of the sides does not fulfill its obligation, breaking the universal principle of *pacta sunt servanda*, doesn't it lead to contract termination?

Perhaps reflections like these led the writers of the Virginia Declaration of 1776 to predict the Right of Resistance, which we transcribe literally:

> "Section 3 - That government is, or ought to be, instituted for the common benefit, protection, and security of the people, nation, or community; of all the various modes and forms of government, that is best which is capable of producing the greatest degree of happiness and safety, and is most effectually secured against the danger of maladministration; and, whenever any government shall be found inadequate or contrary to these purposes, a majority of the community hath an indubitable, inalienable, and indefeasible right to reform, alter, or abolish it, in such manner as shall be judged most conducive to the public weal."

The right of resistance deserves to be considered as an inalienable collective right, as Alexis de Tocqueville (1957: 35) says:

> "No es el uso del poder o el hábito de la obediencia lo que deprava a los hombres, sino es desempeño de un poder que se considera ilegítimo, y la obediencia al mismo si se estima usurpado u opresor.

CHAPTER 7

Fundamental Elements of the Corruption Act

To think of elements, requirements, or assumptions of something is to think of parts that form the "whole".

Corruption is a human phenomenon and, therefore, hungry for the conscious and free volition that drives man to his ends.

A human act is a manifestation of will which, in order to be valued in the juridical sphere, needs to be practiced in a conscious and free way. The will must have been processed by reason (criterion of imputability) and by free will because who acts or omits under coercion is merely the vehicle for the realization of the will of a third party, who is responsible for responding by action or omission.

It is common to say that a valid legal act needs a licit, possible, and determined or determinable object.

In the Brazilian Administrative Law, for example, it is the norm to conceptualize the administrative act as any manifestation of will that creates, modifies, protects, transforms, or eliminates rights.

When compared with the Brazilian Administrative Law, Law Number 4,717/65 (Law of Popular Action), which regulates probity in Public Administration, establishes the following elements of validity of the administrative act:

> "Article 2 - The acts harmful to the patrimony of the entities mentioned in the previous article are void in the following cases:

a) incompetence;
b) clerical error;
c) illegality of the object;
d) lack of grounds;
e) misuse of purpose.

Sole paragraph. For the conceptualization of cases of nullity, the following norms shall be observed:

a) incompetence is characterized when the act is not included in the legal attributions of the agent who practiced it;
b) a clerical error consists in the omission or incomplete or irregular compliance of formalities imperative to the existence or formality of the act;
c) the illegality of the object occurs when the result of the act is in violation of the law, regulation, or other normative act;
d) the lack of grounds is observed when the question of fact or question of law on which the act is based is materially inexistent or legally inadequate to the result obtained;
e) the misuse of purpose occurs when the agent practices the act aiming at a different end from that provided, explicitly or implicitly, in the rule of jurisdiction."

In the wake of what has been transcribed, the valid administrative act is that which emanates from a competent authority, has public purpose, prescribed or accepted legal form, factual and legal motivation, and legal, possible, determined or determinable object. Once these five elements or assumptions are met, the administrative act is considered valid.

Corruption is manifested by typical or atypical conduct, but always contrary to the law or to the moral order established by the legal system. For this reason, acts of corruption should be considered null and subject to administrative, civil, and criminal investigation by the State administration.

7.1 Elements of the Act of Corruption

The act of corruption is born of an act or omission, conscious and free, directed to a certain purpose, such as usurping public goods, diverting or irregularly employing public funds, practicing passive corruption, prevaricating, committing embezzlement, etc.

The active subject of such acts of corruption can be both the public and the private official. The objective element of the conduct of the corrupt, be it active or passive, lies in the action or omission typified in law, and the subjective element in the conscience that deliberately returns to the intended end.

We can say that there are two objective elements: action or omission, expressed in multiple behaviors. There are also at least two subjective elements, such as conscience and free will. As follows:

- **Objective elements of the act of corruption:**

    1 - action proven by law;
    2 - omission not permitted by law;

- **Subjective elements of the act of corruption:**

    1 - the free and conscious will to threaten or harm others;
    2 - the conscious and free omission that threatens or harm others.

7.2 - Internal and External Aspects of Corruption

The act of corruption is thought according to two aspects: the internal and the external.

Internally, the act will be examined within the process of cognoscence and rationalization, both generators of will and free and conscious interest.

Externally, the act of corruption will be manifested by the result produced differently from what the conventions of each society establish.

In the hypothesis of the democratic States, we can say that the external aspect of the act of corruption is the breaking of the law with the consequent imposition of the sanction of such conduct.

It is symptomatic of the external aspect of the act or State of corruption to break the principle of legality, main characteristic of the democratic States.

In Brazil, for example, the Constitution of 1988 in its article 5 says that *no one will be obliged to do or not to do anything other than by virtue of law*. Observe that the law establishes the boundary between the action and the omission legally accepted for life in society. Infringing such rules implies attracting the wrath of the State against the one who committed the misdemeanor. The exception is when the scenario is prepared to circumvent the law, as is the case where corruption has become a system, as is generally the case in Mercosur countries and in countless others where the educational process of the population is deficient.

Guillermo Ariel Todarello (2008: 103-104), in his work *"Corrupción administrativa y enriquecimiento ilícito",* focused on the external aspect of the act of corruption and, specifically in what is committed by a public official. He says:

"De acuerdo con lo expuesto en la conclusión que antecede, y teniendo en consideración la diversidad de definiciones, perspectivas y niveles de análisis que recaen sobre el fenómeno de la corrupción, se ha subrayado la conveniencia de establecer aquellos elementos constitutivos de todo acto de corrupción funcional. En tal sentido, es importante describir la línea de investigación propiciada par Francisco Suarez, quien concluye que un acto corrupto se integra con los siguientes elementos:

- Beneficio: El acto de corrupción administrativa se inicia y desarrolla en la búsqueda de beneficios particulares - pueden ser económicos o no - pero siempre a expensas de un bien público.

- Transgresión normativa: Toda acto corrupto supone la transgresión a una norma vigente. De allí surge la necesidad de mantener oculta dicha conducta irregular.

- Interacción: la conducta irregular al menos dos actores. En la mayor parte de las supuestos, las maniobras se caracterizan par un accionar reciproco entre dos o más sujetos.

- Aprovechamiento de una posición de poder público: En el acto de corrupción una de las partes ejerce un rol de poder, aprovechándose de él al momento de desplegar el accionar indebido.

- Perjuicio: Los sistemas de corrupción pueden desarrollarse en ámbitos públicos o privados, pero siempre implicaran un perjuicio, ya que en todos los supuestos existirá una víctima, aun cuando esta no sea reconocible en forma directa y su perjuicio sea difuso.

- Ocultamiento: Teniendo en consideración que en todo acto de corrupción se observa una transgresión normativa, se impone en forma necesaria el ocultamiento del mismo con la finalidad de procurar su invisibilidad. Este elemento constituye, en definitiva, una de las razones que demuestra las dificultades que deben enfrentar los Estados en su tarea por combatir la corrupción, y ello por cuanto la misma constituye un fenómeno que presenta severas dificultades probatorias, caracterizándose por su rasgo furtivo. Dicho elemento reviste una importancia decisiva ya que el funcionario desarrolla su accionar ilegal en forma oculta, y ello constituye precisamente uno de los obstáculos más importantes para alcanzar su control. Esto permite enriquecimiento ilícito, figura que se hará aplicable cuando el agente exhiba, o demuestre un patrimonio desmedido e injustificado. Tal como veremos oportunamente, esta figura intenta combatir la corrupción desde otro ángulo. Por ello, teniendo en consideración el carácter oculto y velado que presenta el acto viciado, se impone la necesidad de procurar su abordaje a partir del análisis de los bienes que conforman el resultado de dicho accionar ilícito."

Todarello states as external factors:

1 - The pursuit of a benefit;
2 - The transgression of a norm;
3 - The interaction between several subjects;
4 - The abuse of power;
5 - The damage to third parties; and
6 - The concealment, since every transgressor intends to hide his misconduct.

It is important at this point to rephrase the distinction that Mariano Grondona and Guillermo Ariel Todarello made between the act of corruption and the State of corruption.

Mariano Grondona (1993: 22-23) teaches:

> "Por lo que respecta al 'estado de corrupción', existe cuando los actos de corrupción de han vuelto tan habituales que la corrupción se convierte en sistema. En el acto de corrupción se desnaturaliza la acción, pero en el estado de corrupción se desnaturaliza el sujeto de la acción, que en el caso que estamos tratando es el Estado, cuya finalidad – servir al bien común – se desvirtúa, transformándose en el provecho de unos pocos. ( ) Cabe preguntarse qué factores conducen a la desnaturalización del Estado. Creo yo que los principales son dos: el economicismo y la tentación del poder absoluto; La corrupción es posible, en efecto, cuando el dinero ocupa una encumbrada posición en la tabla de valores de una comunidad, y lo cierto es que así parecen estar hoy las cosas en la mayoría de las sociedades conocidas. Lo habitual es que un funcionario viole sus deberes de lealtad al pueblo no porque le prometan un puesto más algo, o por alguna otra condición que no sea económica, sino, porque hay dinero de por medio. Decía Aristóteles que el amor desordenado del dinero hace a veces, por ejemplo, que el médico no atienda a los enfermos para curarlos sino para cobrar."

Todarello (2008: 107,110), in turn, states:

> "Es importante realizar una distinción básica en torno al tema de la corrupción funcional, en tal sentido, debemos diferenciar entre lo que conoce como acto de corrupción y estado de corrupción. En cuanto al primero ya hemos visto que se trata de una conducta que implica la solución irregular de un conflicto de intereses, el cual tiene lugar cuando una persona obligada legalmente hacia un interés ajeno lo pospone en función de un interés proprio.
>
> Por otra parte, cuando nos referimos al estado de corrupción, se intenta caracterizar una situación en la cual

los actos de corrupción se erigen y despliegan de manera habitual, produciendo un escenario donde la corrupción se convierte en sistema, dando lugar a lo que también se denomina sistema institucionalizado de corrupción. ( )

De allí que se haga hincapié en abordar la cuestión a través de una visión sistémica, que contemple todas las facetas del problema social institucionalizado; denunciando que insistir en los actores individuales incursos en actos no continuos de corrupción puede brindar la apariencia de estar atacando al fenómeno de corrupción administrativa, mientras que sólo se está operando sobre una dimensión limitada en el ámbito de lo jurídico. Entonces, mientras se aborde exclusivamente la punición de personas y no se procure actuar sobre la trama de actores y los sistemas relacionados y articulados para el desarrollo de su accionar, los esquemas de corrupción institucionalizados se seguirán perpetuando."

In this work, the same classification sketched by Todarello and Grondona, as to the acts, State or system of corruption is adopted.

The act is represented by action or omission, conscious and free. The State or system of corruption occurs when the active and passive subjects of the acts of corruption interconnect in a conscious and free way for the practice of the crimes and deviations of conduct that harm public revenue.

The act and the State or corruption system make the State administration hostage to the offender's conduct. The tools or instruments of liberation are justice, morality, and law. The problem is that justice and morality always want law, but law does not always want justice and morality.

Reflecting on this, Regis Fernandes de Oliveira, with former vice-mayor of São Paulo (member of the Executive Branch), Federal Representative for two terms (member of the Legislative Branch), and Chief Judge of the Justice Court of Sao Paulo, states (*in* Gastos Publicos, 2012: 76-77):

"The sacralization, first of religion and then of law, leads to the predominance of discourse and the role that each one plays in society.

(…)

Pierre Bourdieu gives excellent analysis on the subject. He clarifies that the performative statements (which send powerful messages) that transmit symbolic domination carry the weight of agents who depend on their symbolic capital, that is, the recognition, institutionalized or not, they receive from a group: symbolic imposition. This kind of magical efficacy which the order or the word of order, but also the ritual discourse or the simple injunction, even the threat or the insult, intend to exercise, can only function as such when fully external social conditions to the linguistic logic of discourse. He clarifies that the performative statement is the legal act that, when pronounced by whoever is entitled, that is, by an agent acting on behalf of an entire group, can substitute the doing for a saying."

BOOK I - FINAL CONSIDERATIONS

We came to the end of Book I of this collection of 5 books. In this first volume, our intention is to offer a historical view on corruption, to conceptualize it, and to study its causes and consequences. We also want to show the profile of the corrupt, to list some of its strongest allies, and to analyze the elements of corruption or its assumptions, humbly aware that a theme like this is inexhaustible.

Thanks for reading. I hope that after reflecting on what you read, you look forward to reading Book II.

The author

Printed in the United States
By Bookmasters